COPYRIGHT © J. A. DAINTY 2023

J. A. Dainty asserts his moral right under the Copyright, Designs and Patents Act, 1988, to be identified as the author of this work.

All Rights Reserved.

No part of this publication may be reproduced, copied, stored in a retrieval system, or transmitted, in any form or by any means, without the prior written consent of the copyright holder, nor be otherwise circulated in any form of binding or cover other than that in which it is published and without a similar condition being imposed on the subsequent purchaser.

FOR DEBS, EMILY, AND HARRY

INTRODUCTION

'The scan showed us that the obstruction is being caused by a mass coming from the direction of the pancreas.'

This is the sentence that turned my life and the life of my family upside down and led me to writing this journal.

This sentence, or ones very much like it, hammer into lives and families on a daily basis and often, like it was for us, they come completely unexpected, and no-one ever totally recovers from hearing it. You may survive it, but you cannot be unchanged from it.

I started to write this journal while still in hospital, as a way to distract me from what was going on and to try to put some order in what felt like an uncontrollable, hot, emotional mess.

I finished it and published it for two main reasons. The main one was to see if it could raise some funds for Cancer UK. Without their research and advancement over the years, the treatment I had would not have been available and I would not be writing this now.

The other? If this helps one person in a similar position to navigate that hot mess a little easier, if it gives one tip that proves useful, or manages to raise the ghost of a smile during their journey, well - it means it was worth finishing it.

CHAPTER ONE

Tis the season to be jolly....

A little bit of background before we get started. Won't take long, honest.

I was brought up in a sink estate called Kirkby just outside Liverpool. It was a poor, hard place with crap schools and lousy prospects.

I managed, with the help of some friends, to scrape together enough qualifications to get me out and into Polytechnic. From there to Cambridge (the City not the Uni) where, after various bar and catering jobs, I fell into the insurance industry.

My first role was in 1989 working for BUPA. Not the most glamorous of jobs, but the branch was moving from paper files to computer records. I was hired to input the senior assessor's files into the computer, which she couldn't do herself because she didn't want to break her nails. (I promise I'm not making this up.)

I moved up to the help desk, dealing with support enquires. Looking back, it was fairly bizarre to be dealing with health insurance claims with an overflowing ashtray on your desk.

Promoted to team leader, I somehow managed to talk myself into a job at Head office in London. Officially creating large corporate reports, conducting analysis, and writing bespoke client contracts. In reality, faking it till I made it.

Made redundant and after a bit of travel, moved to insurance in Folkestone as an underwriter, before heading back to London for my first City job in 1998. I loved it. I gradually worked away from underwriting, towards central operations in large insurers, central services, and the Corporation of Lloyd's itself. This led to designing and engaging with the market on major transformation programmes, including Brexit and more recently a programme to reimagine the central services in the London Market.

It was hard work but a lot of fun and huge sense of achievement. Walking through the legendary Lloyd's doors for the first time was very special - and still is today.

Running alongside this was a personal life that had relationships which were good, bad, weird, and downright scary. There's probably a whole other book in that - but not one I would let the kids read.

This all changed for the better when I met Debs, and we married in 2008. You will be hearing a lot about this wonderful lady as we step through this, as well as our two fantastic kids Emily (13) and Harry (11).

My lifestyle, as this thing started to unfold, was fairly ok, I think. I was exercising a fair amount, but offsetting that with infrequent (maybe once a week?) nights out with friends and work.

We were eating fairly well - just the odd takeaway (but you have to live a little). We certainly were not living off tap water and celery.

Basically, I was a fairly normal bloke working an office job with a happy, settled family.

We hit the Christmas season in the City and if you have ever worked there, you will know it can be a bit of a silly season - just like many other places. You have work functions, team meals, client events, supplier events – the list goes on.

As you get older you try to be a little more selective of which events you attend. Otherwise, you end up living off bacon butties, paracetamol, and caffeine to get through the hangover and on to the next party – that, really, is a young person's game.

Even if you are selective, you can still end up with a fairly packed social calendar and such was the case this year. I had no back-to-backs (too old) and no more than two events a week, so fairly balanced.

I'm pretty sure you can do a solid 20 days of turkey lunches and receptions back-to-back over Christmas, if you have the constitution and the stamina. I say 20, as most people start to drop from sight around the 20th of December onwards.

As the season moved on, I noticed I was starting to get symptoms of reflux, this is when you get acid gas and discomfort, very common. This was not really worrying, I had had reflux on and off for many years, but not much recently. I could usually avoid reflux if I went out for a nice meal only (with minimal alcohol) or just went out for a drink (with minimal food or food afterwards). I am not recommending this approach and sure anyone medical is shaking their head and tutting, but it seemed to work for me.

I just assumed that, as the events usually forced eating and drinking together, the merge was causing the reflux. This being the case, I stepped down some of less essential events and started to guzzle reflux busting Gaviscon – always worked in the past.

But not this time.

I was still in work the last week before Christmas but suffering worse than ever. New territory for me really. I had started taking over the counter omeprazole tablets, which are just the next stage up in fighting reflux by inhibiting acid production in your stomach. Some people swear by them but they did not seem to be helping.

The family of drugs here are Proton Pump Inhibitors which, to me, sounds like something that goes offline at a critical time in an episode of Star Trek only for Scotty to repair them in the nick of time after getting a hair drying from Captain Kirk. We'll refer to them as "PPI" going forward, as there are a lot of different types. Many times, I was not even sure what type I was on anyway.

Clearly the next level of treatment and advice was needed, but getting an appointment with the local GP can be 'challenging' (more on that later). I'm lucky enough to have private health insurance which includes online GP consultations, so decided to give that a whirl.

It was pretty slick with the appointment in a day or so, text reminders and web links - all of which worked fine. The GP took the history and general background, had a good chat with me, and gave her opinion – which was... that I needed to see my local GP, as she suspected an ulcer and recommended finding out what was causing it.

I always thought you got ulcers mainly from a mixture of 'hurry, curry and worry' but apparently that's not the case. Lifestyle can be a contributing factor, but main causes are "Helicobacter pylori" or "H. Pylori" - which is a bacterium. Other causes include sustained usage of inflammatory drugs such as ibuprofen. As my heavy rugby playing days are behind me, I had no heavy use of inflammatory drugs - so felt that the most likely explanation was

H. Pylori.

Tiny issue. You cannot test for H. Pylori if you are taking PPI. You have to be clear of PPI for 2 weeks before taking the test or you can get a false negative, as PPI can inhibit H. Pylori.

We were now only a couple of days to Christmas and as I would not be seeing the GP until the other side, we agreed to stop the PPI now. This way, when I did get to my GP, I would be able to take the test for H. Pylori. So, it was back to Gaviscon for me. Merry Christmas!

CHAPTER TWO

Pardon me vicar...

"Let me see...gunshot wound..., stabbing..., Ah! Here we are, bloody stool - go right through"

It did not quite work out that way.

Just after Christmas a new symptom arrived and if it was a present from one of the family, you would be very disappointed with it. You would hope they still had the receipt. Fair warning as well: During the writing of this bit, I intend to be honest and graphic where required. If it's not your sort of thing, best put this down and find something else to read.

Basically, my poo went black. Jet black. And sticky with it.

When I say sticky, well the stickiest substance on earth is a bacteria called "Caulobactor Crescentus", which secretes a sugary substance so sticky that a tiny bit has the adhesive force of nearly

5 tons per square inch. It was basically that, just slightly weaker. Only by careful management, and having backup rolls of toilet paper used judiciously, did I avoid it becoming a decorative feature across the entire bathroom.

So off to Google I go. Dr Google is another thing that will feature heavily in this, dangerous ground but you have to start somewhere. So, after 10 minutes of dedicated research, it would appear I have "blood in my stool". I'm still trying to decide if that's a good title for a country and western song.

This is not good. At least it appears to be old blood, as it is black. That is not as bad as fresh blood which, unsurprisingly, would be red.

More medical advice needed. This time the NHS 111 service was the option of choice. Mainly as this felt a little more serious but also because the local GP was basically doing emergency cover only and even the Private GP was on holiday. If I did need to go to A&E, better to go via 111 was my thinking.

Got through fairly quickly to a great triage service, which went from the basic "Are you breathing?" and "Is your head firmly attached to your body?" to more focused questions and then the mind-blowing confirmation that the symptoms qualified for a GP chat. Never play 20 questions with these guys. They will fuck you up.

The 111 GP called me back, I gave him the position and he was humming and hawing between 2 courses of action. Option 1: Go to A&E at worst time of year to go, massive wait etc. Option 2: Restart the PPI treatment. At one point he even asked me what I thought. I politely said that what I thought was that I severely lack the required medical school training and experience to have an opinion, so probably a good idea if we went with whatever he felt best.

In the end he recommended I restart PPI that day, at a higher dose, and get to my GP as soon as possible in the New Year. He sent the prescription to my pharmacist and restarting the PPI is what we did.

I managed to get an appointment for the 1st week of January with the GP, or at least a 'potential' appointment. Not sure how your GP service works but I find mine odd to say the least. You cannot book. You have to ring in the morning on a 'first come first served' basis, stay on hold for an hour or so, and talk to someone with no real medical experience about the problem. While they do not have any medical experience, they do have some serious qualifications in appearing bored and letting you know as far as they are concerned you are wasting their time – and the time of the GP.

This would all appear rather useless as the invariable response was being told that a GP would call me back to see if it can be dealt with by phone or face-to-face. Fair play, they do call, and I have had an appointment every time – usually the same day. I am sure this process saves them time or allows better allocation of resource, but for the life of me I cannot see how.

When I finally got to see the GP, he was very, very unhappy. Not with me, my bleeding stools or even his Christmas gift of socks and a tie. He was unhappy that 111 did not send me to A&E when I rang them the first time – very unhappy. If the 111 GP is reading this, I would avoid the dark places on the walk home if I was you. The GP fiddled with the PPI prescription and immediately ordered a priority gastroscopy at the Princess Alexandra (Alex) Hospital, managing to get the 12th of Jan, which was impressively quick. Having blood in your poo certainly opens a lot of doors.

The 12th rolled around, and I arrived in good time for the procedure. Just so you know what this entails, it is basically a camera they shove down your gullet to see what is going on. There are a few tools involved, to spray things or take biopsies, and air is also blown down your gullet to open things up.

You are awake for it, but they give you a sedative which makes you woozy. They also offer you a throat spray, trust me and take it. If they do not offer one, ask for it. The camera is the size of the tube that the face hugger in Alien puts down your throat. Slight exaggeration perhaps but you catch my drift. There is no getting changed into a drafty hospital gown though. Just take your shoes off, hop up on the bed, take the sedatives - and we're off. I have had a gastroscopy before and another two after this one. No memory of anything that happened in any of those but this one for some reason I do remember. Maybe a bit less sedative was administered or what happened during it made me remember, not sure.

There was an ulcer. They found it quite quickly and it was bleeding, so they decided to deliver some treatment while they were down there. I know that one thing they did was to spray it with adrenaline, which helps to stop the bleeding. They also treated it with another drug but didn't quite catch what that one was or what it did.

This mini treatment did not take long but did have some consequences. You see, gastroscopies are only supposed to be short in duration. One of the reasons for this is the air being pumped in is continuous, so it builds up over time, until it needs to come out. And come out it did. I have never made noises like it, it started as a couple of minor burps, but then I started belching from the very core of me – long and sustained, it sounded like a flight of geese, but deeper and louder.

It was scary more than anything. I had, I like to think, a fairly established relationship with burping. I am familiar with it and I can be impressive in the right circumstances. I had no idea someone could make a noise like this and live. They noticed I was in distress; they would have had to have been deaf not to - and brought the treatment to a close, removing the tube.

As they did not want to send me home with the ulcer still bleeding, I was admitted. My wife, Debs, sprang into action as she always does. She arrived with all the necessary toiletries, PJs etc. I was placed on heavy doses of IV PPI to further inhibit acid to allow the ulcer to heal. The stay lasted four nights with the gastroscopy repeated on the fourth day (don't remember that one). As it was no longer bleeding, they sent me home with yet another prescription for PPI. And that was that! Just a follow-up needed to ensure that the ulcer was healed, and everything would be back to normal.

By now, it was mid-January. A few days had passed and it did not feel like anything was healing or getting back to normal. If anything, it was going the other way. The frequency and volume of my vomiting was increasing, so back to the GP. They did not seem overly concerned but simply doubled the level of PPI dosage and tried a different type of PPI. We battled on.

Still not right.

Vomiting was constant now. Usually once, sometimes twice a day, and significant volumes. It never happened before lunch but could occur late into the day or early evening. This seemed to happen regardless of whatever I ate.

After the gastroscopy, I had returned to work. Remotely at least. With the constant vomiting, it felt like I could not really carry even this on. I called Bob to discuss stepping away for a while, as he was running the programme we were working on. Bob is my boss, colleague, and friend. He was fantastic about it, making it clear to put my health first and not to worry about anything else. Bob stayed in contact throughout what came next and is still in touch. Great guy.

At home, I tried to experiment to see if anything would stay down. I tried just protein drinks (nope), just electrolyte drinks (nope) and then just water (and nope). Where do you go after water? Back to Dr Google. Apparently, one of the common complications to an ulcer was a Gastric Output Obstruction (GOO). This is when a blockage forms between the stomach and the duodenum, preventing anything getting through. This felt right and also explained the timing of the vomiting. As I ate, the stomach filled and when it was full or reached a certain level, everything was forced back up. Eating slowly and later in the day meant that it happened later than if I ate earlier. Seemed to make sense.

Worth mentioning at this point that I was starting to lose weight. As for a lot of men my age (56) this was not a problem. If anything, it felt the opposite - to begin with at least. By now, I had lost just under a stone and a half. The GOO would also explain this as food is only absorbed after it leaves the stomach, not in the stomach.

So, what to do next? I wanted to move quickly if it was a GOO as I was getting no nutrients. Deciding to play the private health insurance card, a referral to a consultant at the local private hospital was booked for the 8th of Feb - with the knowledge and blessing of my health insurance provider.

The consultant was excellent. He totally understood why I thought it was a GOO but was not fully convinced. If it was, why had it not shown up during the gastroscopy? Midway through the consultation he stopped abruptly. He wanted to see if he could get me on his list that Friday. Today was Wednesday and he knew he had one slot left. I was lucky enough to get in.

Now the fun really starts…

CHAPTER THREE

Care out of the community

"Would Sir be having the chicken or the fish?"

10th February
Day 1

IV Fluids

'It looks like we were both right, you do have a full obstruction'.

That was the first phrase I can remember the consultant saying as the gastroscopy sedative wore off.

The gastroscopy, although in a much nicer environment, was a similar affair as the ones in the Princess Alex. the drugs worked on this one, so no real memory after they put the sedative in, although the outcome was very different.

The consultant had found a full obstruction near the top of the duodenum. When he said 'we were both right' he was referring to my thoughts that there was an obstruction and his belief that it should have shown up on the previous gastroscopies. It did not show up because it was not there when the original investigation was done. This obstruction was above the ulcer, so must have formed since the first gastroscopy.

This put certain wheels in motion. I was told 'I could not stay in the community' as, with the obstruction, my body was not getting any nutrients at all and very limited hydration. There was a bit of 'no shit Sherlock' at this news. Perhaps that's why my weight had dropped massively and my fingers looked like they've been in a 9-hour hot bath....

Have to say, not staying in the community had a nice ring to it. I felt like I was some sort of gangster being taken out of circulation and put in some form of protective custody. Alas it just meant that, not being able to feed myself, hospital and medical feeding was needed. Would there be a menu? Will it involve a blender? And/or a pump? Will there be a choice of red or brown sauce...?

So it was back to the Princess Alex, as the Rivers hospital could not give this sort of treatment privately. We had been prepared for this outcome and Debs was again on standby with a bag of essentials and the motor warmed up.

The only way to get admitted was via A&E. The consultant did as much as he could to smooth the transfer, warning the gastro team to expect me and putting together a small pack covering a bit of the history and the results of the gastroscopy. This included six pictures taken during the procedures, one of which showed the obstruction. To me, they just looked like a set of Yorkshire puddings that had gone seriously wrong.

Debs came and got me, and we set off. Debs wanted to stay with me but Harry needed looking after. Emily had set off that day for a week's holiday with the school and, even with the consultant's introduction and pack, it was now 4 o'clock on a Friday. Admission via A&E could take some time. Debs dropped me off and in I went.

Reporting at reception, I tried to explain they were expecting me but this did not really fit their process. The pre-admission work only had limited effect, which was sort of expected. The gastro team were off shift by the time I passed reception so no assistance there either. The consultation report did have some impact though - some good, some bad. More of that later.

I had entered the A&E mill and settled in for a bit of a wait. One of the 'essentials' packed was a Kindle, as this was not my first rodeo. Triage process kicked in and everyone, including me, seemed to be seen quickly for base line observations, heart rate and blood pressure. This makes sense, as those seriously off are probably the folk you want to get seen fairly soon. My observations were fine, so back to the main waiting room and my Kindle.

After an hour or so, they called me up to a window to ask for more history. Surely the chap had the information available as it had been given a couple of times now. Maybe he just wanted that personal connection or, long shot, did some of the systems not really chat to each other? You guess.

This time it seemed to stick and the next time I was called it was to see a doctor and a junior doctor and they already had the gist of my position, although we went through it again. Just for shits and giggles.

These guys need to make decisions quickly and I was not disappointed. The decision was to admit me and, in the interim, fit me for some IV fluids and a Gastro Nasal (GN) tube. With that, the doctor was off to the next one leaving 'junior' to sort the treatment out.

Now just hold on one goddamn minute, IV fluids I get - but GN tube? This is a tube that goes down the nose into the stomach. Clue is in the title I suppose. It can be used to feed you or remove stuff from the stomach rather than vomiting it up if you are having problems with either of these actions. They are a bloody awful effort to get in place. No nice sedation or throat spray here, tube is shoved down your nose and you must try to swallow it as it passes the back your throat, while trying to ignore the intense gag reflex.

I could not see how it was useful for me right now. It could not be used to feed me, my stomach was obstructed so anything they put down the tube would sit there until it came back up and even if it was not obstructed, I was fairly good at getting food into my stomach the traditional way. A process known as 'eating'.

Were they putting it in to take material out of the stomach? As I was not eating anything there was nothing there so what would they be bringing up?

Now you have to realise, I was getting a bit weak. Weight loss and dehydration were slowing my mind - as well as being sedated that day. Before I had properly thought it through, Junior had the GN tube out of the pack and was enthusiastically entering it into my nose.

I had a word with Junior, several words in fact. I was just really trying to understand what it was going to achieve. The response was that 'doctor' had said I should have it, but that was not good enough for me. I pushed. I needed the *clinical* reason. What good would it do?

This caused a bit of confusion to be honest, with him just repeating it had been recommended by the senior doctor and he had opened the packet now, so might as well?

The tube was down my nose by now and approaching the back of my throat, so I pulled it out and advised that the patient refused treatment. Maybe that made things easier for him.

It did and with a sad look, a sigh, and a slight shake of the head he gave up and passed me onto a nurse to sort the IV fluids. I found out later all the NG tube palaver came about because my private consultant mentioned in his handover pack that I may need one 'in the future'. A lesson to be careful of throwaway comments being written into treatment plans - be on your guard...

I realise now I could have handled that one a bit better. After all, Junior was just doing his job and trying to help. However, I really do not like those NG tubes at all. They make a repeat appearance later, and karma is certainly a bitch.

Anyway, I was on to the next station and a nurse fitted a canula for the IV fluids. If you are not sure what a canula is, it's a line inserted into your vein and left there to allow multiple drugs to get into your system without making separate injections. Nurse did a first-rate job, straight in and IV fluids connected in double quick time. The move into hospital was starting to feel real. I was led around the corner to a sort of waiting area. It was now around 7pm.

This felt like a sad, bad place to be. There were quite a few people (Twenty? Thirty?) already there, the number ebbed and flowed as the evening went on. Injuries and illness are not always easy to see, but you could sense that some of these people - maybe a lot - were in a very bad way.

Some had family with them, most did not. Hushed conversations and words of encouragement and query was the main background music here. People were pretty much wrapped up in their own concerns and probably, like me, wondering what was coming next.

At one end of the room there was a desk with a couple of nurses behind Perspex and down one side of the room were treatment cubicles equipped with curtains that people were called into from time to time.

The final stage of the wait began and went on. Looking back at this, I should have realised that any admission was going to take time. It was Friday night in A&E, that would be enough on its own. There were a lot of people, many who seemed in a worse way than me, and let's assume beds were limited.

At the time, I did not really get all of this. I was feeling weak by this stage. Due to the obstruction, nothing I had eaten for the last three to four weeks had been absorbed, so I'd been living on water for nearly a month. I was also getting very tired, not just due to the lack of food but also due to the gastroscopy and sedative that morning.

As time progressed, I became more tired and started to feel a bit 'spacey' and started to disappear into myself. I could not read anymore as the words were not really making any sense and the pages were sliding away from me.

By about 10pm I was asking how long it would be. Even as I was doing it, part of me knew that they were going as fast as they could and moving people in the most appropriate order, but the logical side of me was in the minority. The emotionally controlled side of me was getting in the driving seat and I did not like it.

Later I asked if I could just go home and come back tomorrow. I realise that does not probably make much sense but by this stage I just wanted to sleep so badly. I could see myself whining and was not happy with what I saw but could not help it.

They came for me just before midnight. By this time, I was doing a fair impression of a nodding dog and feeling fairly miserable. Into a wheelchair, followed by a brief memory of corridors and lifts. I ended up in the Adult Assessment Unit (AAU) where my bed awaited. I remember taking a picture of the bed to send to Debs, so she knew I had landed. Kicking off my shoes, pyjamas on and then not remembering much else…

Day 2

IV Fluids
IV PPI

Woken up around 6am, mixture of things really. The ward itself was coming to life with nurses bustling around starting to take observations, patients starting to move and talk, the main indicator was the lights coming on. This was probably one of the longest sleeps I managed to get during my stay.

The AAU was a holding position really, so I was expecting to move to another ward soon. Possibly by Monday or even over the weekend. In the meantime, treatment started. They put me back on fluids and pushed through some PPI. Anything else was going to wait until we knew what the treatment plan was going to be and I suspected that plan would not be set until Monday.

Spoke to Deb and put in my shopping list which was just me filling in the gaps from the bag I had with me. I am a bit of gadgetophile so needed a lot of tech: Kindle for books, iPad for films/boxsets, headphones and sleep headphones (headphones built into a headband so you can sleep in them - another godsend for hospital). Sleep was going to be a major factor in the days to come.

The rest of the kit was toiletries, PJs, and clothes. Clothes because I wanted, if possible, to avoid just staying in PJs all day. I wanted to get up have a shower and get dressed every day I was in as it felt that the routine would help.

The move actually happened pretty quickly - classic NHS. The first I knew about it was a porter turning up and getting a bit grumpy that I was not ready – no biggy, shoved stuff into a bag and off we went to Harvey Ward.

I ended up spending quite a bit of time here, so worth explaining the set up. Harvey ward was basically a corridor with rooms off the left and right. Most rooms had four beds in. Mine had two, as did a couple of others, and there were a couple of singles. As far

JOE DAINTY

as I could make out there were two actual nurses to cover all this, supported by nursing assistants with others covering portering, cleaning and getting meals out. I was in one of the rooms near the bottom of the ward.

Still hooked up to IV fluids and getting PPI once a day, I spent the afternoon watching the rugby. Ireland continued their run and Scotland had a memorable victory over Wales. To be honest, my old school 1st XV could have given Wales a run for their money at this stage.

Debs came in and we went to the coffee house so I could watch her drink a coffee. I was nil by mouth due to obstruction. Debs was not wanting to get anything else in sympathy with me but I persuaded her to get a muffin, so I could at least smell it.

It was a nice break of scene from the ward. This meant I had to be unhooked from the IV, but as the bag ran for 12 hours, 40 mins was not going to make a huge difference.

Box sets took up the early evening and then, changed back into Pyjamas, sleep. Another full night and awoke just before 6am, too much banging about and lights coming on. A morning alarm that was to become routine.

Day 3
IV Fluids
IV PPI

Sunday was fairly quiet. PPI in the morning, more fluids. England beating Italy. Debs coming in and cheering me up. She brought Harry with her, who did not share his mother's attempt at solidarity with my no eating effort and happily tucked straight into a brownie in the café without any form of persuasion.

Two of my cousins came along. Fair old distance for them, halfway around the M25, so was very grateful. This was the first inkling of how much support I would get during this from family and friends. Debs had also brought in my sketching stuff, as I wanted to see if I could use the time here as usefully as possible.

Back upstairs and alternating between reading and watching more Netflix / Prime / Disney +. Bedded down early again.

At this stage following a couple of good sleeps I was feeling fairly good. I was not in any pain, just feeling a little tired and weak. At this stage it was easily manageable. Now it was just about waiting for Monday to understand the treatment plan. What were they going to do to clear the obstruction?

INTERLUDE

Sharp Scratch Index

You will be hearing 'sharp scratch' a lot during any hospital stay and it pays to give this some of your attention. It is obviously covered in the NHS training handbook at all levels, as you will hear it from anyone who wants to stick any form of needle into you.

But while the phrase seems to be universal, the experience is certainly not. Some are just the 'sharp scratch' they propose to be while many are absolute mother fuckers, causing a level of pain that if someone on the street inflicted it, they would be up for assault with a deadly weapon.

Let's try to put a scale on it should we? Welcome to the scratch index.

At the lowest end of the scale is **glucose blood sampling**. A small tool nips a bit of skin off a finger. Never any digging about or missing veins, so it's quick as well. The only thing to watch out for is the nurses tend to have a favourite finger, usually the middle, so encourage them to take more of a selection box approach or you end up with one finger black and blue and the others looking smug.

The next is **blood sampling**. This is still at the low pain end of the index, especially if taken by one of the 'professionals'. They are focused on this day in and day out, with their own blood cart and everythin'. They are straight on you, twisting your hands and arms, tapping, knocking, wiping, and muttering about relative value, deep veins, scar tissue etc.

These guys are one shot experts, they could get blood out of a mummy. Need to be a little bit wary if anyone else is trying, for example junior doctors, although I have been asked by John (Family MDT – explain later) to stress anaesthetists should also be considered experts here as well, so not to feared.

Don't get me wrong, there may still be a great deal of enthusiasm from the amateurs but results can be variable. Some amateur blood collectors do not have the instinct to hit the jackpot. Rather than a precision strike it is more like pin the tail on the donkey, hoping that one of the strikes will eventually bring it home. My record was four tries on a single hand.

Multi-strikes are usually narrated with a nervous level of technobabble around how you have specific blood giving issues, low veins, deep veins, sluggish blood, or circulation, post operative impact and so on. All bullshit.

Frustration can set in, and the scratch can start to feel like they are trying to take a bone sample rather than blood. You almost imagine them looking you in the eye while they screw the needle in and down, saying 'how do you like them apples?'.

I am sure it's desperation rather than malice. Well, fairly sure. It can be corrected with a well-placed sucking in of breath and a 'steady chief!' – or similar warning of your choice - which should hopefully get them to reset the mining operation.

To help them out, and to try to increase their strike rate, try to guide them to happy hunting grounds the experts have been using.

Moving up the index we arrive at the **insertion of a canula**. This can be relatively painless if completed by an expert but can have the same problem as blood sampling if conducted by amateurs. It is further up the index as the guide needle used to place the canula is longer and has a wider bore than blood sampling, so if someone does get it a bit wrong it bloody hurts. You don't really want someone digging around too much with this one.

There are also only specific areas that cannulas can be fitted. The main ones are the crooks of your elbows, backs of hands or sides of hands or forearm. You can run out of sites quite quickly. As the options decrease, more tricky sites can be explored. This can increase the level of digging to hit a vein significantly, along with the associated groans of pain.

Last on the index are **subcutaneous injections**. This is a broad church. Some are not painful at all, on par with glucose sampling - but some really, really are.

If the sharp scratch statement is accompanied with a 'now deep breath in' it is going to fucking hurt, a lot. Sometimes the deep breath statement is omitted, maybe they do not want to spoil the surprise, so treat all injections with suspicion until you know for sure one way or the other.

I had an enzyme injection one which felt like they were pushing liquid magma into the vein, it hurt like a bastard and caused involuntarily swearing.

CHAPTER FOUR

All good stories have a twist

"In the curious case of the vomiting insurer, it quickly became clear to me the culprit was not the ulcer, nor the obstruction. The actual villain is...."

13th February
Day 4

IV Fluids moving to IV TPN
IV PPI
IV Antibiotics

Awoke to the increasingly familiar bang and crash of the dawn chorus around six. Got up, naughtily disconnecting myself from the IV, to go and have a shower and got dressed. Ready for another day of, well, sitting around really.

Debs was in touch seeing if I needed anything. As this was half-term, she was trying to juggle me in hospital with doing things with the kids, but was dealing with it like a pro. I ordered some more tech, mainly chargers that I had missed. I had also ordered a massage gun which I asked her to bring in. This became another life saver further down the line.

She had some good news too. A holiday company had agreed to defer our holiday which we could not go on. They did not need to do that according to the terms and could have just kept the money. Just shows that not all companies are bad.

The lead nurse told me the consultant rounds would be sometime before lunch, so I settled in to wait. I had consulted Dr Google and thought I was looking at maybe a course of antibiotics to help take down the inflammation and if that did not work, a balloon angiogram. This is a small balloon passed down the throat and inflated at the obstruction to open it up, or maybe even a stent, this being a rigid tube inserted into the obstruction to hold it open. We will see....

The consultant came around just before one. Lunch was just a time marker for me. The next time I would eat or even drink anything was still over a month away. It was a team of three, led by the consultant. Then what seemed to be a senior junior doctor (usually a registrar I am advised), by this I mean a chap who really seemed to know his stuff and did a lot of the talking but deferred, heavily, to the consultant. There was also a junior doctor who usually piloted the Workstation on Wheels (WoW) and took notes.

The 'WoW' is a piece of kit that seems to be ubiquitous in hospitals and used by all. WoWs are linked hospital terminals where you can record information and call up drug information, patient history, test results etc. They ran on battery so were mobile when needed and could be plugged in if anyone wanted to work stationary.

According to John (you will meet him soon, honest), they used to be called "Computers on Wheels". This practice was discontinued after phases such as 'can you wheel the CoW in from room 4?' were misconstrued once too often. WoW it is.

All the information was uploaded to all WoWs as soon as it was input. Seemed like a really good piece of kit, state of the art, and this made it all the more difficult to understand how the information was so often missing and or simply fucking wrong.

So let me get this out the way.

This record is in no way meant to 'bash the NHS'. Nearly everyone I met was trying their best and genuinely cared about the patients and was doing an excellent job in often difficult circumstances. The problems seemed to me to be around two main areas: A lack of trained, skilled staff; and patients being a pain in the arse. Both areas will be covered later.

That said, there were some areas that were not great and I will call them out if only for anyone who ends up in a long NHS stay - with or without major surgery. It may help to know a few things to look out for and I am not ashamed to say, sometimes you just need to vent....

Back to the consultants round, pleasantries were exchanged and down to the matter in hand. To be honest the first session was a bit frustrating, they did not seem to have all the history, so we went through that again and somehow, they had a record of me being asthmatic. I am not and told them, but it would take several repetitions before it actually made it to the WoW. Not sure it ever did properly.

So we went through the history, they consulted, throwing the odd question at me, and then wandered off with smiles and junior doctor tapping away furiously. I was not sure what we had agreed, if indeed we had agreed anything. There was a discussion of a CT scan 'soon', some IV nutrients 'almost definitely' and 'probably' IV antibiotics.

I started to learn that you need to ask very clear questions and push to get clear answers if you wanted to know what was going to happen. Not to say they were not doing the correct course of action at the right time, but if you want to know what it is, you need to ask very clearly and hold on until you get an answer.

The lead nurse cleared most of this up after she came around following the consultant round. I got the impression that this was a regular translation service. It was not uncommon for people to be unclear about what had just been agreed on so the nurses would, diplomatically, fill in as many of the gaps as possible - all whilst just 'happening' to come around directly after the consultant.

For me this was to confirm that I would be put on to IV antibiotics and nutrients later that day and a CT was being organised, date/time to be confirmed.

Debs came around in the afternoon and we took up our usual spot in the Costa. I gave her an update, she, wisely, was asking all the questions I did not, when was the CT? When will they start the IV drugs? Anything else planned?

As these were all very sensible questions, I obviously snapped at her, saying I don't know, place is chaos, I tried but did not get answers, and other such protestations. Very much displaced frustration. In my defence, but not much of one, was the usual tired and weak position. I did apologise shortly afterwards, albeit by WhatsApp. Debs being the much better person in all circumstances, she rose above and started talking about the rugby. Very safe ground.

Back upstairs after an hour or so and after dinner service, treatment kicked off with the fitting of IV drugs.

The antibiotics were fairly straightforward, IV fluids off, canula flushed and on with the antibiotics. There was a bit of a caution from the nurse: 'This antibiotic is quite strong, and some people do have a bit of a reaction to it'. This turned out to be a typical medical understatement.

Then the IV nutrients were put on a separate canula as it needed a dedicated site. It is called TPN, which stands for 'Total Parental Nutrient'. It is balanced in such a way that if for whatever reason you cannot eat or cannot process food, it acts as a complete nutrient and fluids substitution. This would hopefully stabilise my weight going forward, until the obstruction was resolved.

It is a big plastic 'shopping bag' of several litres of fluid and is given over a 24-hour period. This means you are now wedded to the IV stand, as you cannot disconnect until it is finished. It is tricky stuff in a number of ways. You cannot risk infection when it is being connected up, so has its own sterilised kit and separate gloves to connect it up. It is quite caustic so if given via the canula, which I was, it tended to 'burn' the surrounding tissue and cause local pain and swelling. When this happens the cannula site is blown and another is required to be set up.

It was quite thick and white in colour. For the Sci-Fi buffs out there, it was like getting a blood transfusion from one of the androids in the Alien films. If this does not mean anything to you, then it looked like milk.

So ready for sleep with 2 lines in my left arm, one in the elbow and the other in my hand. CT scan, I assume, would happen tomorrow......

Day 5
IV TPN
IV PPI
IV Antibiotics

Awake to the clattering of pots and pans, not a good night's sleep. The TPN line had the tendency to set off the pump pressure alarm quite regularly, which scared the shit out of me when it first went off. After a while, I learned to reset the alarm myself as it was not worth ringing the nurses' bell so they could 'switch it off and on again'.

They did not like you doing this. On the other hand, I did not like waiting 45 mins in the middle of the night for someone to press three buttons to reset it. I saw it more as assistance than resistance.

The IV PPI was run through, then the antibiotics. Neither took much time. The cannula site (for antibiotics) was starting to go red and swell so probably need a new site tomorrow.

Previously I said I wanted to get dressed each day but not being able to disconnect from the TPN meant this was not really possible, so hoped to get 30 minutes between changing TPN packs to have a shower and change my T-shirt at least. The TPN still had 15 hours or so to run, so I made do for the moment with a full body flannel wash and cleaning my teeth - the new morning ritual.

Got a lovely message from Debs wishing me a happy Valentine's Day, which I promptly responded in kind. Luckily, I had used the internet wisely a few days ago so chocolates and flowers had arrived in time but I think she would have given me a pass this year if they hadn't. We don't do a lot for Valentines, but both feel a little gesture is appreciated. Sometimes I do go a bit silly but not this year.

Started waiting around for the CT scan, only to be told just before midday that this would not now be going ahead until tomorrow. A lot of people may find this frustrating and some even get angry. I do get it though. This hospital had a busy A&E department and would, I am sure, be constantly going through a triage process. Getting 'bumped' is just part of that.

The annoying bit is more around the team not passing the information on. It was often the case that the team would know something was not happening or even had confirmation when it was going to happen, but advising the patient could be a bit hit-or-miss. More often it was miss. In fact, quite often.

With no CT scan, back to what was becoming a normal process: box set, reading, listening to audio books, watching people eat. It did feel a lot more restricted as constantly plumbed in to the IV stand for the TPN.

Debs came up around 6pm, suppose I could have gone down to the Costa with the IV stand, but it just did not seem worth the effort. My shopping list for Debs was modest now as I had got nearly everything over the last couple of days, just a couple of T-shirts and a pair of reading glasses as somehow, I had knelt on the pair I had. We had chats about everything and nothing, as you do.

Was settling down for the night by 10pm. I had managed to agree with the nurse, when she was removing the TPN bag, to give me 30 minutes to shower and get changed. This perked me up quite a bit, back to bed and hooked up to the next 24 hour 'nosh bag'.

Although disturbed, this was probably the last night of anything close to a full night's sleep I was going to get until I was discharged.

Day 6

IV TPN
IV PPI
IV Antibiotics
CT Scan

Today everything changed. It would never be the same again.

Up and over to the bathroom for the one arm wash and brush up. My scan was scheduled for 9.40am. These timings were for guidance usually (reasons given above) but this time it happened pretty much spot on.

The porter and wheelchair arrived just after nine. The IV PPI and antibiotics had gone through, so, just had the TPN. As suspected, the antibiotics had blown the cannula site and the back of my left hand was swollen and red. Another cannula site was put into my right hand and it looked like the TPN site was going the same direction.

Anyway, got on the wheelchair and given the TPN bag to carry. This was not one of those little IV bags you see on Holby City but a massive bag in another bag (TPN does not like sunlight) carrying several litres of milky liquid. As I could not be disconnected it was coming along on my lap for the ride.

Wheeled across and down via the lifts to the imaging centre, left me feeling like a patient probably for the first time. It is quite a vulnerable feeling getting wheeled around in your jim-jams with an IV fluid going in. You see people's view softening in sympathy and/or trying to ignore you. Not in a bad way, it felt more like trying to give you some space.

I have had CT scans before so knew what to expect. It went off without any real incident. The only tricky bit was getting on the bench without accidently disconnecting the TPN. Once we had worked out the logistics of this the scan happened, so back onto the wheelchair and back to the ward. One thing I did find a little amusing was the contrast between the level of technology.

The CT scanning room was a modern delight with its blinding-white huge pieces of hi-tech machinery, complete with sound effects. The wheelchair was the other end of the spectrum. It looked like it had seen service between the wars, with more loose fibres than Bagpuss and it had to be pulled backwards rather than pushed due to a dodgy wheel.

I did not get a consultant round in the morning as they were waiting for the results of the CT scan to help them decide the best course of action. Until then, we were to continue with IV drugs so no need to discuss.

The team came around 2pm with the results from the CT scan.

Usual team structure: Consultant; Registrar; and junior doctor piloting the WoW.

After a few pleasantries, they moved on to the results of the CT scan. The registrar was leading and, at first, I did not understand what was being discussed. They seemed to be moving around a topic and I could not work out what it was. It all seemed a bit disjointed. They started to see my confusion, so the registrar tried another tack.

'The scan showed us that the obstruction is being caused by a mass coming from the direction of the pancreas'.

There it was. The left field sentence that was going to change my life and the life of my family.

The registrar was still talking, with contributions from the consultant, but I cannot remember what they said. I don't think I really heard it to remember. I had gone. Somewhere else.

I find it really hard to describe my reaction to the information but will try. Once I had comprehended 'mass' the rest was less rational and more instinctive, more emotional. At the time, mass meant cancer and cancer meant dying - probably soon.

My mind then seemed to over clock on what will happen to me. Was I going to be able to leave the hospital or would I die here? Probably die here but do not want to do that, could they look after me at home? I wanted to go home.

Was it is going to be painful? Definitely. How long? Probably not long. Could they be wrong? No.

How can I tell Debs? The kids? The family? I can't.

Does this mean they cannot remove the obstruction? Probably not, so will I not eat again, ever? Maybe not.

All of this was happening in microseconds. Thoughts surfacing, disappearing, and being replaced by others. Each bleaker than the last.

I so want to say I was like one of those people in the dramas. You know? The type who accepts the news with quiet grace, understands there are options and vows to fight hard. Not me. No. I was in free fall.

I say 'dramas', I am sure there are people in the real world who can handle news like this with a form of calm acceptance and a balanced view of the options. If there are, I am in awe of them. I am certainly not one of their number.

I think it was the 'C' word and its implications that caused this - to borrow from the Dexter novels - 'dark passenger' that had taken me over. An older emotional response to the news, one which could only think about the worst.

I do not think it was the sense of dying itself, or not only that. I have, on a few occasions, had the misfortune to look closely at my mortality and the good fortune to evade it. None of them hit like this.

A few years ago, I had a post-operative arterial bleed following an adult tonsillectomy. By the time I got to hospital, I had lost a lot of blood and they were really struggling to stop the bleed. By the time I was being treated in A&E, I crashed. My overriding memories before I lost consciousness was someone shouting, 'His blood pressure is in his boots!' and a nurse desperately squeezing the IV bag to try to get fluid into me.

When I came around, they were getting an ENT surgeon to blue light to the hospital I was in, as I was too ill to move. I was prepped and wheeled into emergency surgery to stop the bleed. They had managed to halt it briefly but it had already restarted.

While I was being wheeled towards the operating theatre with Debs following, the anaesthetist stopped the trolley and asked me 'Do you not want to say goodbye to anyone?' I thought then this was it, I got off the trolley hugged Debs, told her not to worry and that I loved her and the kids. She responded the same while telling me I was going to be fine. I smiled and got back on the trolley and on through the doors. I could handle that with some level of dignity and control, but not this. Not 'the Big C'.

Thinking about my physiological reaction, I would liken it to cold water shock which I have experienced a few times in my life.

In cold water shock everything else ceases to matter, the cold owns everything for as long as it lasts. This was like that. Cancer owned everything. I do not remember feeling anything else, I had no sense of surrounding, I was crying without being aware. I think my mouth was trying to shape words but not sure.

Not sure how long it lasted, I had lost sense of time with everything else. After a while, I started to make out some of the words that were coming from the registrar and consultant, it was like background noise in a bar - sometimes you can work out words or phrases if you concentrate. It was not 'fading in and out' but more like my attention was wholly elsewhere, apart from odd moments.

The gist was they were telling me that they did not know what it was. It could be a cyst or something else. It did not mean it was cancer. I was ignoring that. My dark passenger had already decided it was cancer, with the worse possible outcome, and was showing no signs of shifting that opinion.

They were also telling me they were not expecting to see the mass, so the CT will need to be repeated to get a picture of the whole mass and this would be done tomorrow. To be honest, I did not catch all of this at the time and filled some in from later conversations. I was still in shutdown.

I must have said something, not sure what it was but bet it did not make much sense. Eventually they left and Anna, the lead nurse on the ward, came in. I needed to do something. I needed to try to swim back into some form of normality.

I asked her to unhook the TPN. It still had hours to run but Anna, seeing I was in a lot of distress, did not put up much resistance and removed the feed. Anna, I was to find out, was a lady with a lovely soul and high amounts of genuine empathy. I did not know how working on the wards did not break her and others like her, but she was there for me when I was the most frightened and lost. I will always be grateful to her for that.

I had a shower. It was autopilot. I thought a normal activity will help me to start functioning again. It did to some extent, a very modest extent. Some thoughts of 'what to do now' started to creep in alongside the cycling of bleak consequences.

I realised I needed to speak to Debs, and started to think how the hell I would do that. The dark passenger side was still in control. Firing up Dr Google only fanned the flames of my despair, detailing what an absolute bastard pancreatic cancer is. Less than 10% of people lasted more than a year – TEN PERCENT!

Part of me knew I was basing all of this, including Dr Google, on almost no information. But that part of me was firmly in the back seat and could not be heard over the radio.

I called Debs, don't remember exactly what I said. I know I told her not to come in, which was ridiculous, and I could not really stop crying. This effect lasted a few days, I could not speak to anyone about this without tearing up. It was an involuntary action, like shouting 'ow' if you banged your head.

Even now after months, I can find myself getting emotional much easier. Not just about this. I think this experience has permanently shifted my emotional responses, brought them closer to the surface, which may not be a totally bad thing.

Anyway, Debs of course ignored me and called back telling me she was coming in. I was relieved. I was not yet capable of thinking of how hard this was going to hit her or the kids. My response was still fully focussed on me, I am ashamed to say, and I wanted to see her. I wanted, needed, some comfort.

I had to kill some time until she arrived, so tried to read, or watch the iPad, maybe listen to music - but what was the fucking point? That sounds melodramatic and it was. Nothing I could do about it. Trying to do anything just triggered a feeling of futility, which caused the bleak thoughts to cycle and the tears to come. I ended up passing the time, and it was hours, just staring into space trying with variable success to keep my mind as empty as possible.

Debs texted me she had arrived; I went down to meet her. We met in reception and went outside. We knew, instinctively, that the next bit was going to be hard so decided to go and sit in the car for some privacy.

We were there for over an hour, and I am grateful we had each other. Some people have to go through this shit on their own, that must be a whole new level of hell. We helped each other face up to the facts, we were both still leaning towards the worse possible outcomes.

Debs was trying to put some other more positive options in there, but they did not really make the cut. It is instinctive, I think, for people who are close to the epicentre of news like this to assume the worst - at least initially. The more positive vibes are reserved for people a little further away from the blast.

There were tears, a lot. There were sentences that did not finish but we knew where they were going. There were many silences. There was much comfort.

There were some decisions. We decided we would be honest with the kids, as we have always been, however we would not be talking about the Big C until it was certain. While my conviction was in place and, to be fair, I think Debs was there as well but we should not mention it to the kids until we were certain it was. It needed to be fact, not fear.

We also decided that we needed to get more information and try as best we could to keep a rein on the base emotional response until we knew more. This would be easier said than done. We reaffirmed that we were in it, whatever it was, together.

We said our goodbyes and I headed back to the ward. I felt a lot better thanks to Debs - still scared shitless as well as a bit lost and unsure of what will happen next, but better. I also think that the intense emotional reaction I'd experienced at first just cannot be maintained for a long period of time, it is too big.

I was still cycling the bad thoughts and outcomes, just at a lower level. Some more positive possibilities were starting to butt in, to balance things a little.

Back at the ward more staring into space I am afraid, still working through options, outcomes and 'what ifs'. Slightly less desperation than before but still pretty grim. The passenger was still firmly in control.

I got a message from Debs to say she had told my sisters, as we had agreed. Following this they were both planning to come down the next day. My sisters are a force of nature (in a good way!), and we will cover them in detail later, but at that moment I could not really handle it.

I did not want to see anyone. I begged Debs to tell them to hold off till we knew more or, in reality, till I could somehow get my head around this, so I could somehow start to deal with it.

She contacted them and they agreed to hold off for the moment, I think they understood. I hope they did. It was only a delay of a few days, but I was not in a good place right then.

It got late, so I went to bed. Pretty sure they refitted the TPN, but it did not really register. Same for a new cannula they must have fitted, as it was there in the morning. The lights went out and I settled in for a long night.

There was only one thing for it, I needed to contact John. I will need to explain who he is.

I've known John for practically all my life, certainly most of it I remember – primary school onwards. We were very close as children and young adults, we are still very close now but in a different way. He moved to Australia in the 90's so the relationship has shifted, but not broken.

He is the smartest person I know. For some, that might not mean much but I know a lot of smart people. Honest.

I have mentioned how crap the schools are where we lived. In fact, when they first did UK school league tables, the borough I lived in – Knowsley - was bottom of the national league. And our school was the bottom in the borough. We were literally the crappest school in the UK.

Despite this, John got straight A's at O-Level; straight A's at A-Level; and was the first student in the school's history (40 years or so) to go on to read medicine - which he also passed with flying colours. If you do not know what an 'O' Level is – Google it. He is that smart.

Even while he has been halfway around the world, we have stayed close. Until the pandemic we would see each other on average once a year, memorable Lions tours of Australia and New Zealand amongst them. I could always trust John to give an honest appraisal of anything in respect of medicine, especially if I was in a panic - such as when Debs was in a lot of pain after the birth of Emily. He was my go-to.

It made perfect sense to get his help, and not just because of his clinical knowledge. I needed to talk to my best friend.

The time difference worked in my favour here and we started talking around 10pm UK time. First, I let him know what was going on with a rambling description of what I knew and telling him that I was terrified. This was not via voice, as call is not our preferred communication method. Either face-to-face or

WhatsApp were the way we rolled.

He came straight back with what I hoped he would, obviously he was upset but also started laying out that the cause was not cut and dried; laying out what the causes could be; and layout out that we needed more information.

This was all done in his usual completely honest style. There was no 'it's going to be alright, don't worry' here. He did offer to call, a clear break in protocol, but I could not. I was still in shock and could still not talk about this without bursting into tears.

We swapped messages. John was pointing out cancer was likely but it could also be a cyst, abscess, or pseudo cyst. It was understandable to be scared but I needed to try and get my brain refocussed on practical matters. In his words to 'keep the lizard brain fucked right off'.

We signed off around 11pm but I was back messaging him just before 5am. He explained if it was cancer, what would happen next and what tests I should be looking for to determine if it was or wasn't. These conversations were the single biggest reason, after Debs, for me starting to get back to any sort of even keel.

It was a refreshing wash of no-nonsense opinion from someone who knew their stuff, was not trying to avoid any of the conclusions and not trying to handle it with kid gloves and platitudes.

It made it practical. The humour also started to creep back in. At one point I wanted to ask him if it was cancer and had spread, did he think I would get out of hospital before I died as that was the one really bothering me. Below is the exchange that happened.

> There is a question that is rattling around my head and I will ask it I know it is too early etc but will ask as the real one keeping me awake 05:25

Is Santa real? 05:26

> Too early 05:26

Sorry 05:26

> 😄 05:27

He is tho 05:27

By the end of the exchange, I felt much better and more importantly the blind panic and storm of thoughts had calmed. I was starting to allow logic back in. It may not be the Big C and even if it was, there would be options.

The dark passenger was starting to move towards the back seat, swapping places with a more logical driver, but it felt like he could still lean forward at any time to fiddle with the radio.

CHAPTER FIVE

*Multi-Disciplinary Teams,
everyone should have one...*

Dainty MDT – **ASSEMBLE!**

16th February
Day 7

IV TPN
IV PPI
IV Antibiotics
2nd CT Scan

Obviously did not get much sleep, so gritty and tired. CT scan was being repeated this morning, focussed on the mass rather than any ulcer or inflammation. That was past now. Debs was in touch early doors, sending me pictures of the kids asleep and the dog out on his walk, normal stuff but really nice to see.

The ride to the radiology suite was not as carefree as the one yesterday, it had a lot more riding on it. I was pretty silent, still wrapped up in my own thoughts. Debs and John had helped a lot but I was still prone to wandering dark areas in my thoughts.

The scan was uneventful, same faffing around with the TPN and positioning but if there was a difference between the two it wasn't noticeable to me.

The response was noticeably faster this time, we had definitely upped a gear. The consultant team came up around 11am. They must have been waiting for the results as soon as they became available, which was reassuring.

It was a big mass. About 6cm tapering to 5cm. They confirmed it was a lesion not a water filled cyst, this removed some 'more favourable outcomes'. They would not be able to confirm whether it was cancer or not until they managed to do a biopsy and that was going to be difficult given the obstruction, they could not say how, or when, they would be able to do it.

While they were keen to point out that we did not know what it was, I felt they did think it was cancer. This may have just been me and where my head was, but I don't think so.

Certainly, they had to treat it as if it was cancer and were trying to hold a delicate balance between sending me off the deep end by confirming probably cancer, while treating as such and keeping me positive by saying it may not be. I had already pretty much decided it was, although my chats with John had taken the certainty out.

They were keen to point out everything they saw on scan indicted the mass was discrete, everything they could see indicated it has not spread beyond the pancreas which is very important if it was cancer. Regardless of the cause of the mass, the best outcome would be to remove it - if it could be removed.

What I was really looking for was a plan. That was the way I was built: A to B to C. Frustratingly that was not where we were, given the mass I was to be transferred to a multi-discipline team (MDT) to consider the next steps and this team did not meet until the following Wednesday. Six days away.

I realise now that this time frame was reasonable. The referral makes perfect sense and in the context of treatment I was being referred to the MDT and on the agenda for the very next meeting, so very quick.

It did not feel like that at the time, it felt like a Big C clock was ticking and if I did not get instantaneous treatment and a clear plan, then the opportunity to treat it would be lost and I would die - which was crazy. However, crazy is what I felt. The passenger was starting to lean forward.

I needed the biopsy NOW. I needed the plan and the date for the mass removal NOW. I tried to get the urgency and sense of doom I was feeling across to the team but crying kicked in again so not sure how much I got across. Not sure how much it would have changed anything if I had managed better anyway.

The meeting tailed off; not sure anyone was happy with outcomes. Only one thing to do, back on the phone to John.

I gave him the update and he helped me unpack it. Yes, probably was cancer, but not definitely yet - still some other options. He explained that MDT was the way to go and also explained ok to question and push the treatment plan. The more involved I was, the better. It was ok to 'kick up a fuss' and discuss options, he was surprised I had not done this already.

I was not in this place at that time. I was weak, tired, emotional, and scared. I could not pull myself into a place where I could debate and influence treatment approach. He got this and the key thing, for me, was to conserve energy and try to stay strong. But we still needed someone to manage the treatment side, Deb had her hands full with the family and supporting me. Then, I had an idea.

> Seriously. Your job is to get
> some nutrition in you and
> conserve energy   12:03
>
> 👍

> Might tag our Janet in 12:03 ✓✓

> You wanna be walking around
> (DVT risk) anyway. Bound to
> see something....   12:04

> Forgot about your Janet.
> Fuck yeah. Weaponise that
> motherfucker. SHE was built for
> this   12:04

So better explain who 'Our Janet' is – welcome to the sisters of mercy.

I have two sisters, Polly and Jan. Our mother passed when we were fairly young. I was in my twenties, and both my sisters are older than me - with 4 only years between the three of us, me the youngest and Polly the eldest. Polly took on the role of 'mum' following this, at least for me. I would spend Christmas and some holidays with her, and her kids. Jan was more often there than not, later with her kids as well - and we are all very close.

Jan was always the strong willed one of us, she did not take any nonsense and if she thought something was wrong, she would challenge it and challenge it full on. She has been a nurse since her early teens and remained in the NHS until a couple of years ago, spending the majority of time as a ward manager. Some people may think of her as 'hard' (she hates this), but she is not. It is just mis-labelling a strong strength of conviction. I have to say that - or she will hit me.

She will fight for what she believed was right for herself or for her family and friends – she is a doer.

We are very lucky to have a very strong bond, don't get me wrong - we have our moments. But nothing to threaten the love we have for each other. It was not so much about bringing them in, rather it would be impossible to keep them out....

In effect, we were forming our own multi-disciplinary team. Debs was overall co-ordinator, with special responsibilities for family, friends, and work communications - as well as being Chief Morale Officer. Jan would be in charge of hospital and treatment liaison; Polly would be supporting both Jan and Deb, in morale and family communications - and John was our consultant referral. He is family really. His wife Gina was already in contact with Debs offering help and support as well.

I checked with Jan if she was happy to talk to the medical team on my behalf and she jumped at it. I gave her what details I had and she was off to talk with them immediately. She was going to focus on making it clear that we were looking at swift mass removal and understanding the best route to get there.

It may be the case that the treatment I received would have happened the way it did without the family MDT involvement, but I strongly suspect it would not. Without doubt, if it was not for the Family MDT and the support it provided, I would have broken emotionally and mentally. I cannot thank them enough. I really can't.

Debs came in around lunchtime. Jan had already spoken to one of the doctors, possibly one of the registrars, and had an update. She had impressed on them that the focus should be on mass removal, it needed to come out whether it was cancer or not. She was also able to give us a bit more of a layman's understanding of what they had spoken to me about earlier in the day. Jan was definitely on the case and was lobbying hard.

Debs had started to tell family and close friends about the change in course, I had also sent a message to Steve advising the mass had been found.

Steve is someone I have worked with for years and is a very close friend. We have been through some shit together and we are all the stronger for it. He does not take much nonsense but also is the first person to stand up for anyone - and I mean anyone - that is being bullied or picked on. He is a natural protector. He is ex-military, and this might be evident by his response when I told him I had a mass that may be cancerous.

> on my head. Just checking with Royal Free as the experts that it can be removed, they meet on Tues. Not sure what we do if they cannot excise it but will stick with plan A till it is not
>
> 18:35 ✓✓

Mate. 18:36

I'll cut the fucker out. 18:37

> Rusty tin? 18:37 ✓✓

With anything. 18:39
😂

I am lucky to have such friends. He joined the family MDT acting as "London Market Liaison". His primary task was keeping the team I worked with updated on progress. Almost all of them had been in touch, wishing me well, asking me how I was doing – they really are the best bunch of people. The amount of support they provided throughout this was humbling really. Like I said, lucky to have such friends.

I asked Steve to update them as, while I was getting more in control, I was still struggling with it all and if I tried to speak to them all individually, I would break down. I was operating on minimal emotional bandwidth.

Steve also updated various people in the market who were asking after my health, the amount of interest would have been overwhelming even if I was not a bit 'fragile'.

I also told 'Texas Pete' what was happening. Another work colleague who I've known pretty much since I joined the market. Top bloke. He is the one who goes and gets a shovel, if you tell him you have a body in the car.

Obviously kept (Wild) Bill informed as well. Again, I've known him for many, many years and he is practically family. Had to be a bit careful with this as he is a qualified (US) surgeon. Any sign that the treatment was not going as he expected, he would probably appear over here in scrubs carrying a scalpel. There were others that have been so supportive and kind but better stop there – starting to sound like an Oscar acceptance speech.

Talking to Debs and doing all the updates pretty much finished me off. I still could not focus on films or books so just put the bed headphones on with some music and fell into an uneasy, short sleep.

Day 8

IV TPN
IV PPI
IV Antibiotics

I was awake well before the dawn chorus. Sleep was getting more and more difficult to come by. Some of that was due to the worry but generally sleep, for many, is hard to come by. I was starting to feel gritty and slow; sleep deprivation was going to be one of the biggest problems overall with an extended stay.

Observations still being taken every four hours. I made a mental note of them and passed them on to Jan, so she could tell me anything I should be worried about.

My control was starting to come back, but still could not talk to anyone outside the family without choking up - even with family it was difficult. I still told a few people via text, but mostly leaned on Debs and Steve to update people.

During the day I did have a mini breakdown. I was worrying about how the kids would cope if the worst happened. Anna was there to comfort me, reminding me we don't know what will happen and there are always treatment options. I do not think she knows how much her presence helped. It really did and would not be the last time she did this.

Debs had taken Harry to the cinema, and they came in afterwards. This was a real test for me. We had agreed to tell the kids together about the mass, so could not do it until Emily was back on Sunday. We had to keep the conversation light with Harry, when all I wanted to do was hug him as hard as I could and tell him everything was going to be ok. Really telling myself I suppose. I still do not know how I managed it, but he seemed ok when he left.

Debs was still dealing with all the other stuff like a legend: updating people; moving/cancelling holidays; starting to liaise with my work; continuing her own work - don't know how she kept it all in the air.

Had a weird episode during the changing of the TPN bag. The 24-hr timeline usually gave a switch over early evening. Up to now, I had managed to have 30 minutes or an hour during switch over. I would have a shower and, if time, a quick walk around the hospital car park just to get some fresh air. Made me feel less like an inmate. The nurse who was exchanging tonight was having none of it. "Old one off. New one on!" She would not entertain a gap at all. Not sure if she had just had a shit day, wanted to finish her shift, or felt this was the best way to do it – probably a combination of all three. Anyway, straight off, straight on.

I tried to ask for a gap, if only to have a shower. I am afraid I got a bit emotional, not that it made much difference. Even the bloke in the next bed shouted, "He is only asking for a shower, for fucks sake!".

She was not having it and started getting the new bag ready. I tried a different tack, could I not have a wash and change my top? She could see I had a point here, as bag change was the only time I could change my top. At least I could have a quick wash as well once the bag was off. This nurse was made of sterner stuff. Instead of taking the old bag off, letting me change top and then putting a new bag on, she changed the bag, then took my top off, passed the bag *through* it (remember this is a big thing, several litres), then threaded the new T shirt through the new bag – how bloody pointless was that?

If I was in a better state, I would have not let this happen. To be fair it was practically over before I knew what had happened. She was the only nurse that, before or after, did not leave a gap. Bizarre. Jan went mental when I told her later.

Day 9

IV TPN
IV PPI
IV Antibiotics
IV Paracetamol

Weekends are generally a bit quiet in the Hospital, especially in the Princess Alex. Consultant rounds only happened during the week so there were no changes to treatment usually.

Mid-morning, I did get a worried junior doctor come down to see me on his own. Didn't think they were let out unsupervised, maybe it's a weekend thing.

He told me they were worried about my bloods, especially the level of bile salts in them. He asked if I felt itchy. Did I? I may have a bit. 50-year-old blokes are always scratching something or other and now I was not sure if I was feeling itchy just because he had asked.

I answered with a safe "Maybe but not much". He assured me I would know if I felt the level of itching he was referring to, something to look forward to then. He left advising me to let the team know if I became itchy or my eyes started to turn yellow – I assured him everyone would know if either of those things happened.

The likely reason for the increased bile salts in my blood is the mass was now pressing the bile duct which stops the salts from entering the duodenum, so they were backing up into the bloodstream.

This would be resolved by surgery, so now something else rested on the deliberations of the hospital MDT. If not surgery, they would need to empty the bile duct and address the gastric obstruction.

What I was noticing was a growing level of abdominal pain. It started as discomfort but was increasing in intensity. I was put on IV paracetamol to take the edge off and it seemed to do the trick, so was having that every six hours.

I was losing canula sites fairly regularly. TPN needed its own dedicated site, the new TPN bag they put on early evening did not last long. The cannula site became swollen and red after 3 hours, so they had to take it back off. I was also losing sites as the antibiotics were fairly toxic, so caused problems.

By this stage I think I had lost about 7 or 8 canula sites and they were running out of options. They were going to have use my feet soon if some of the previous sites could not be reused, as the swelling was not going down fast enough. I was being considered for a PICC line for the TPN, whatever the hell that was.

The TPN being taken off gave me some unexpected freedom, so went for a shower and a long walk around the car park before heading back to the ward.

Able to read again but not for long, so it was another long night with not much sleep.

Day 10

IV TPN
IV PPI
IV Antibiotics
IV Paracetamol

Emily arrived back from skiing late last night. Debs was coming in this afternoon with both of them and we were going to tell them things had changed. We had discussed and agreed that, whilst we would do it together, I would try to lead.

I was really nervous about this. I had gained a lot more self-control over the last few days, but the control was fragile and still a tendency to well up when trying to talk about my position. I was hoping I could hold it together, as it would be hard enough for them without me losing it.

Debs was still updating various family and friends, at the same time asking them to direct all queries to her as not ready, or able, to talk to anyone outside immediate family.

I did feel a little selfish about this. These were people, and so many people – more than I would ever imagine, who were just concerned about my well-being and wanted to know how I was and if they could do anything to help and here was me refusing to speak to them.

It would not be too long before I could talk about it but, for now, too hard. This was mainly self-protection but there was another reason. People do not know what to say when they hear you may have cancer and they can be left feeling helpless, especially if the other party is a blubbering mess. Much better for all if I spoke to them once I could do so in a way that was not going to cause more distress.

The pain had taken a sharp uptick and sleep was hard to come by. IV paracetamol was every six hours, but the effect seemed to be wearing off after 4 hours or so.

Debs was in the car park and on the way up. We had timed the visit so it was in the middle of pain relief, to avoid them seeing me in pain. It also meant I was as clear headed as I could be.

They came in. Emily was full of stories from the ski trip she had been on and Harry had tales of what he had been up to, mainly trips with Debs when she could fit them in.

We moved on to the update. We decided long ago, like most

parents, not to lie to our children and this was not going to be an occasion when we broke that. At this time, we were not sure that it was cancer. My unreliable emotional response was that it was, and the team seemed to be treating it like it was, but nobody was certain.

We told them what we actually knew. There was a mass on my pancreas that was causing the obstruction, and the doctors were deciding if they were able to remove it. The shock and concern on their faces I would have given anything not to see. It came very close to ending my control there and then.

They had few questions at the time: When will they decide if they remove it? Soon, probably before the end of the week. What will they do if they cannot remove it? A difficult question, but fairly easy to answer. We don't know and we are expecting (hoping may have been better) that the mass can be removed.

Emily did ask if it was cancer. She had done some fund raising for stand up to cancer as she loved the bake off, so the question was not unexpected. I told her we simply did not know yet as it was very early. She did accept this, which was a relief, and it was the truth.

The visit came to a close fairly soon after this. We reassured them as best we could that the best team were doing everything they could to help me get better, and we would tell them as anything changed. I could see them taking it in and being so brave nearly broke me. Such strong kids, they take after their mother.

Jan was still calling and pushing the team for the MDT decision and talking to the doctor about the blood results. She was also starting to push for a PICC line – I discussed it with her and she advised it would be much easier for TPN and nothing to worry about.

I was told that the antibiotics have been discontinued, which made sense as this was originally meant to treat an inflammation that we now know is not there. Also told I would get a PICC line put in tomorrow, sure Jan did not influence this at all……

Day 11
IV TPN
IV PPI
Morphine injections on demand

Pain really starting to bite now, paracetamol not really doing the job. They reviewed and decided to stop it - not just because it was not handling the pain but also because of the liver issue. I was switched to subcutaneous morphine on demand, with a minimum 4 hours between doses.

This sort of scared the shit out of me. Morphine is a big boy drug and I had horrible visions of leaving hospital concerned about nothing except my next fix. Did not need to worry, I didn't notice any 'high'. It did deal with the pain but I did not need a clock to know when 4 hours had passed.

Not much happened really, in a holding pattern waiting for MDT decision. Jan continued to push on this and getting the blood/liver results. The insertion of the PICC was delayed, it would probably happen tomorrow.

Had my usual shower and walk between TPN shifts. Lack of sleep was starting to bite, energy levels were falling, and I was starting to get a bit foggy. Thinking processes felt like they were slowing down and finding it much more difficult to concentrate, so glad I had the family MDT team on the ball as I was a bit useless.

During the evening I rang the bell for pain relief. A nursing assistant came in, switched off the bell and said, "Nurse on way". 30 minutes later there was no sign of nurse and the pain was building, so pressed the alarm again. Different assistant; bell off; "nurse on way". 30 minutes later and I was in the foetal position on my bed moaning in pain.

I had not appreciated how much the morphine was masking the

level of pain I was in, I knew now. I am sorry to say I lost my hospital manners. Severe abdominal pain will do that.

As the nursing assistant came in to switch off the alarm - and no doubt tell me nurse was still "on way", rather than mumbling thanks (which I and most of us normally do) I led with "Do not switch that fucking alarm off unless you are carrying a syringe with morphine in it". This was not received very well. She reached over to switch the alarm off and I repeated the message, with a little more volume and more inventive swearing. Alarm stayed on.

The nurse duly arrived and gave me the shot, I was crying with the pain by now. He was really, really apologetic and meant it. It was not his fault at all, it was not like he was hiding around the corner having a fag.

I found out later, that as morphine is a controlled substance it needs sign off by two nurses and to be administered by one. As there were only 2 nurses on the ward it takes time. This goes back to one of the main issues not being a lack of staff, but lack of *qualified* staff. They can get a fair number to switch an alarm off, less so to administer treatment.

The trick is to keep an eye on the time and call early. Assume it takes an hour and you will be about right, a lesson learned the hard way.

CHAPTER SIX

You seem to be a good candidate, but do you have any relevant experience?

"That was great, can you just take us through your pancreas exercise regime again?"

21st February
Day 12

IV TPN
IV PPI
Morphine injections on demand

D-Day.

Today the MDT team should be telling us if I was an option for surgery. This was a major thing. If I was not and it was cancer, then the outcome would be 'sub optimal' and I was back to a 10% survival rate over a year. It does focus the mind.

The consultant round happened in its usual formation, not much to cover. Minor discussion around pain relief and liver function, confirming MDT decision expected today. I repeated my mantra of being ready for surgery, confirming I was fit, resilient, young, sexy, suave – anything that made me look a better candidate really.

It did feel like a competition, one that I really did not want to lose. It wasn't really, looking back it was really about the medical position. I do think the work Jan did with the team, trying to be positive and reinforcing that we really wanted the surgery and were fully prepared, played its part.

WhatsApp was very active between the Family MDT, passing along updates. I was having a few issues with noisy neighbours especially during the night. Jan, being the healthcare professional she is, offered to put a pillow over one of them and Polly, another dedicated health worker, suggested swapping name tags so the other patient got the morphine which might shut him up. Polly was also asking what a 'bustard' is, I explained it was a bastard with extra spell check, bless her.

I had ordered some noise cancelling headphones and Debs brought them in. These were a real help, the ubiquitous curtains did not provide much sound proofing, and my other headphones did not block the incessant noise. I knew nearly as much about my neighbours' medical position as my own, I certainly know what TV channels they preferred.

Received a good reminder that 'it is not all about me'. Emily attends a music theatre group which she really throws herself into. Debs told me she had been given quite a prestigious regional award, so proud and a great lift to the mood. Certainly the best news I had had since I had been in here.

The surprises continued to come, as the team came to fit the PICC line. Like me, you probably have no idea what a PICC line is so a little background. When I first looked into it, it looked blood scary to me. Still does to be honest.

Basically, they insert a thin tube under local anaesthetic into a vein in your arm and then thread it through using ultrasound to guide it up inside the vein to empty out in the vein just above the heart. That does sound scary doesn't it, or is it just me?

Burrowing into a vein all the way up your arm and down your chest to your heart, just feels a bit major. Something that should be done in a bright antiseptic theatre by begowned practitioners - not with me flat out on my bed trying to hold still while the 'Bargain Hunt' theme music drifts in from the next cubicle.

As per usual, they know what they are doing and I need not have worried. Sterile pack was laid out; machine positioned; local anaesthetic applied; and we were off. After the needle, there was no sensation at all and in very little time we were done.

I was congratulated on having 'excellent veins' and it is surprising how proud you can be of something you have absolutely no control over whatsoever. They also fitted a PICC line to the guy next to me, this took three goes and I can remember feeling smug due to my vein prowess.

This PICC line was used for my TPN feed and made things so much easier. TPN is caustic and was one of the main causes for me starting to lose potential cannula sites. The PICC stopped this, so reduced the number of cannula sites needed.

This was just as well as, if it had continued, they may have started looking for sites in my feet. This is sometimes referred to as 'druggie' sites, as commonly used for habitual drug users whose arm veins have collapsed.

I finally got the news I was waiting for late in the afternoon. I saw the registrar coming around the corner and prepared myself the best I could. This hopefully would set the course of my treatment for the rest of my life.

It was good news, but as with anything vaguely related to complex NHS treatment, was not definitive and still had some question marks - some of them serious.

The Royal Free team had confirmed they were 'leaning towards' removal of the mass. I waited. There was obviously more. BUT... They wanted to do a PET CAT scan in advance, which is a scan that looks for 'unusual' cell activity in different areas. Sites that have high activity usually, but not definitively, indicate cancer.

Took a me a while to piece everything together but as I understood it, the picture was this: The mass was almost certainly cancer. All the scans so far indicated it had not spread, and indicated this strongly, so removal was possible. But there was a better scan - a PET scan - which would be able to show much more clearly if there was any indication of spread.

If it had spread - depending on how and where - it was entirely possible, if not probable, that the removal would not happen. If that was the case, we were very much back into sub-optimal outcomes. I was shooting for the moon here. A reality shock I got was learning that less than fifteen in a hundred in this position actually go on to have the mass removed. Fuck.

The conversation moved towards logistics. The Alexandra did not have PET capabilities but the Royal Free did. The team at the Alex wanted to get the transfer sorted then sort the scan, but it was unclear which way the Free wanted to go. Transfer 'likely' to be arranged and may be as early as tomorrow.

Jan, the family MDT medical liaison rep, will sort out all of that. Gave her a call later and she was all over it, working with the team to influence transfer first and scan second. Her thinking, probably not wrongly, was that the decision to go ahead with removal may not be binary. It may live in the glorious medical neighbourhood of 'opinion'. If we do end up in a position where the choice between removal or not is balanced, it is more likely to go ahead if I was already in a bed making spaniels eyes at the consultant.

I settled back with the TPN pushing through the new improved PICC line, wondering if there was anything else I could do to make

Day 13

IV TPN
IV PPI
Morphine injections on demand

The change of diagnosis was starting to get around and Debs was throwing a lot of time at friends and family liaison. Until now, I did not think I had a lot of friends - a mixture of being male, my background and, well, I can be a bit of an arse.

Maybe it takes something like this for you to realise how many people actually do care for you, want to know how you are - and want to help.

I'm not sure I thought about it much really. If you had pressed me, I would have thought I could count friends on the fingers of one hand. Turns out I would have to take my shoes and socks off, and still be nowhere near finished.

Speaking to Debs, hearing what people were saying and getting messages directly, the concern and the hope I get better was humbling, emotional and uplifting. Knowing so many people cared gave an extra boost to keep pushing and helped - tremendously - to keep my dark thoughts and dark times in check.

We received flowers from my team, from work, from close partners I worked with. We received books from many people, thoughtful books that showed people knew my interests, along with cards - countless messages of support and offers of help.

A lot of people wanted to come and see me but I could not really cope with that, not now. My control was improving and fairly balanced between good and less good outcomes. Seeing people outside of immediate family, I felt, could break that balance.

I know from experiences on the other side of illness, it is difficult to know what to say when you are visiting, especially if the Big C may be involved. You want to be upbeat and say, 'you got this' and 'you are strong, you will get through this' but the truth is you don't usually know enough to know if this is true, or even likely.

I will let you into a little secret. The person who may have the Big C does not know what to say either. If they are like me, they will try to reassure you everything will be fine as they do not want to distress you and that can be very difficult. Especially if you look like shit, which I did by this stage. Much lighter than they would have seen me last, tubes everywhere, in my Jim-Jams with patients moaning all over the place with one of those patients being me.

I asked Debs not to arrange any visits for the moment, and hope people realised it wasn't because I did not want to see them. It was just too hard to do for me. I did not want to cause any stress to them either if I lost it.

The relocation discussion to Royal Free rumbled on, along with the 'how and when' of the PET scan. Jan was looking after all of that and doing it as only she could. She was updating us on a regular basis, seemed that it would take a couple more days to sort itself out.

The waiting and the uncertainty were hard, but nothing could be done that was not already being done. A lot of it was down to complex points about availability and triage of things like bed space and ambulance transfer services. I do not envy the people who need to make these sorts of decisions for a living.

Day 14

IV TPN
IV PPI
Morphine injections on demand

Pain control continued to get harder to manage, especially at night. I did not end up in the level of distress I had been in previously, but pain was a fairly constant worry now. The morphine was still doing its job, however the period at the end of the dosage before the next one was becoming more and more uncomfortable. I could feel the block slipping away and the pain creeping back in, leading to an anxious time till the next dose was applied.

As the dosage was every four hours, it also meant my schedule pretty much revolved around it. This also meant I could not get more than three and half hours sleep, increasing sleep deprivation. This is not just feeling tired, but also slowing down like a descending fog on mental capability without really realising it. Almost like being drunk but without the fun bit first.

It is just not nice to be so dependent on something, sitting there watching the clock till your next 'fix' is just bloody horrible. If your 'dealer' is delayed, you are trying not to whine but feel a little ashamed of yourself when you do.

Anna came around to see me with the big news of the day, the Royal had confirmed that the transfer to them would happen as soon as a bed and transfer could be arranged.

I was going to be on my way then, and a step closer to the operation I wanted to have desperately. I messaged the family MDT and called Debs. We tried to keep our excitement down as there was still a real chance that the PET scan could still change the course of treatment, but we will take the good news for the moment. There had been precious little of it over the last couple of weeks.

Jan now changed approach to talking to the teams to expedite the transfer, she really was a machine in this area. She was talking about mental health impacts, clinical outcomes, all sorts of stuff - best I kept out of it.

Anna was also pushing the bed manager at the Alex and the Royal Free. She went above and beyond, as did many of the team.

A lot is said about the NHS, some of it in this journal, but the overriding experience is just people doing their best in difficult circumstances while being a shining example of decent, caring people.

To celebrate, Debs planned a little surprise and arranged a reunion with the only member of the immediate family I have not introduced you to, Herbie the soppy labrador.

Under the cover of darkness, she brought him in the car and, during a TPN bag change, I went down to meet them in the car park. We opened the hatchback and there was an explosion of tail, ears, fur, and tongue, all spinning around in a confined space.

It was lovely, I used that voice that you would be arrested for using on anything other than a dog (whooseagoodboooy!!!) accompanied by random tail thumping, licking and more spinning. Of course I was crying.

He calmed a bit down after a little while, I took a bit longer. The three of us sat there, Debs and I talking about the developments of the day and the latest well wishes from people Debs had spoken to, while stroking the dog who was cocking his head between the two of us as he followed the conversation. Less spinning but still thumping.

We stayed there as long as we could, eventually after a final hug for Herbie and a kiss for Debs, I set off back to the ward. My TPN beckoned.

Herbie was probably wondering what the hell was going on - this was not a walk, so what the hell was it? Why did dad look and smell so odd? Where is my biscuit? and other such doggy thoughts.

Anyway, it was great to see him. A sharp taste of a home that I missed so much after weeks away. Weeks that felt like months.

Day 15
IV TPN

JOE DAINTY

IV PPI
Morphine injections on demand

I had long hair and it was pissing me off. I should put that in context. I had long hair for a 50-year-old male, which is to say I had a short back and sides with the fringe a bit long. For reference, it was not even reaching my eyebrows.

Currently, I was still managing to sneak a shower and a walk during the TPN bag switch. I might not be able to continue this if I went for the op, or if treatment changed. I still wanted to hold on to showering and changing for as long as I could, it was still important to me. I think it showed I was still in some form of control; I had some form of routine that I was still in charge of. I had not given up and settled down into the bed to let things happen to me.

Long (very relative) hair would make that washing hard if I needed to move to one handed flannel washing, which seemed likely in the future especially as the transfer had now been confirmed. Debs and I discussed the possibility of getting a haircut.

Now, we could have just mentioned I was going off to get my haircut to the ward team and the response would have almost definitely been a shrug, indicating to get on with it. They had better things to worry about, but where was the fun in that?

Debs spoke to Kristy, who does a bang-up job of her hair on a regular basis. She was willing to do mine and so, Operation Jailbreak Haircut was on….

During TPN switch over I had my shower as normal and went for my walk meeting Debs in the car park. We set off towards home. Home, there was a thought. I had been away now for over two weeks, so much had happened during the period it felt strange to be going back.

I am not going to say 'it was two weeks but felt like months' as that is not exactly right, it did feel longer, but it was more around what home was based on had fundamentally moved. Pretty much everything we had planned, everything that was important had shifted, rearranged to allow for the diagnosis and treatment.

It affected everything, of course life was going on but there was no area that had not had to alter to accommodate the requirements of the mass I carried inside of me. I was looking forward to going home, but in the back of mind I knew it was a different home to the one I left.

We pulled into the drive and the house was in front of us. We are very lucky to live in an old, thatched cottage. Over its 400 years, it will have seen things that make our current situation the smallest blip on its history. That was ok, the permanency of the building itself gave comfort.

Getting out of the car I realised how much I had changed. I was dressed in jeans, t-shirt, and fleece. The jeans were large for me now, held on by a belt utilising the first notch, rather than the last. Same with the T-shirt. XL previously, I was a large at best now. It would have been flapping around me if not for the fleece.

I was gaunt, unshaven with black circles under my eyes and cannulas hanging out of my arms and hands. I was solemn, unsteady, and slow as I walked towards the door. I had not really noticed how much I had changed in hospital. Now at home, the deterioration was stark.

I said everything had altered but that was not quite true, Herbie hadn't. The door opened to an explosion of dog, showing me his favourite toy for approval, wagging his tail so hard his back legs were lifting off the floor and jumping up. In my state, nearly putting me on my arse. They say have a dog and you will always have someone happy to see you come home. Good old Herbs.

It was lovely to be home. The familiar sights and sounds were just comforting, but it did feel strange at the same time. Partly because of the shift I mentioned but also, I knew I couldn't stay. I was just visiting and had no idea when I would be back for good. That was hard.

Kirsty arrived just after us and set up in the kitchen. She and Debs bustling around setting things up with bright easy conversation and plenty of laughs, it was like a breath of fresh air after the confines of the hospital.

Before I knew it, I was in the chair with a cloth around me being asked me what I wanted. That was easy - as close to a buzz cut as Debs would allow. She did not like my hair very short, but on this occasion, she allowed it.

All too soon, what little hair I had was on the floor and it was time to get back in the car to head back. I look back at the trip as a warm light in a bit of dark time, despite all the changes and shifts - both in the situation and in myself - it was great to be home even if only for an hour or so. Thanks Kristy.

Day 16
IV TPN
IV PPI
Morphine injections on demand

It was going ahead today.

Anna had just spoken to the Royal and they had a bed with my name on it. She was just sorting the transport, which could be anytime but probably this evening.

During my stay, I only had one visitor outside the family - Dom. We are very close to Dom and Keren, and they supported Debs and I so much during all this. I know I said I did not want to see anyone outside the family, but he and Keren were so involved that they were the exception.

Dom is a ball of energy, so much so that I am often worried about him. He is either running a marathon, half marathon, bike ride, big swim, preparing for something - or recovering from it. Thank God he doesn't take it too seriously and still knows how to enjoy a pint.

He was his usual irrepressible self, straight into finding out how I was, cheering me up, sharing stories and giving me updates. I didn't need to worry about becoming emotional, I didn't get the chance.

He had brought me a couple of books about cycling, right in my sweet spot, and then with a smile, a hug, and a wave - he and Debs were off. Debs had to get back as she was taking Ems to a West End musical, still making herculean efforts to keep normal life flowing for the kids while balancing everything else.

Transfer was to be early evening: I was packed and ready to go. Felt a bit weird going to a new hospital, bit like 1st day at a new school. Would I fit in? Would the layout be similar? Would the teachers be better or worse? Wasn't worried about bullies taking my lunch money – no use to me.

The ambulance driver, Terry, arrived. Straight away got the impression here was a nice bloke. He was older than me with an easy smile and a gentle manner.

He got me onto the wheelchair, one of the extremely rare ones that you could push forward, and we were off.

I felt I had achieved full patient status now rather than 'just visiting'. I was thin, had 2 drips on the go, a massive bag of TPN, shorn hair, stubble and two blankies - one for legs and one for shoulders. Yep, bona fide patient right there. I could have only looked more like a patient if I was out front wheeling my oxygen tank, while having a crafty fag.

We got to the ambulance and I found out I was the only person being moved. Terry had actually finished for the day before this trip and had agreed to do this as a favour, got the impression he did quite a bit of that.

JOE DAINTY

He got me in and strapped to the chair, then got into the cab, put the heating on, checked if I needed anything and we were off.

It felt very cosy, cocooned in there in the dark, with the heat blasting out and a bit of an adventure after being stuck in the hospital for nearly two weeks (not including the haircut jailbreak).

I am not usually a big talker in cabs, which this felt closest to, but it was natural with Terry. He was local to the Harlow area, and we had an easy conversation of which bits he knew and the history of them and him.

I joined in with the little I knew and spoke about where I lived and my family. He went through his job, how he loved transferring people and things between hospitals, mainly on his own schedule. He seemed very satisfied with his lot. He recognised his work was important and had a deserved sense of pride in it.

Eventually he turned on the radio, just low in the background and I watched the wet dark streets slide past as we started to head towards West London.

After a while, we started to approach Hampstead where the Royal Free is located. "The Free" was a little outside Terry's usual round but, after a few false starts up and down a couple of residential streets, we pulled up outside the Royal Free.

The Royal Free was founded in the late 1800s but the current incarnation was built in the 1960s, and as per most building of that time it featured concrete and plenty of it. Not pretty in the slightest, a big sprawling concrete box, but if it can get the mass out it will be the prettiest hospital I know.

Terry booked us in and after a few minutes the side door opened and there was a porter with a wheelchair. I said my thanks and goodbyes to Terry and was off into hospital, backwards. It seems the quality of wheelchairs in the Alex and the Free were equally shit.

68

I was taken to ward 9, my new home – no pissing about with ward names in the Free: 9th floor, ward 9. Betcha some image consultant is still spitting feathers about this.

It was quiet and I was put into bed with a minimum of fuss. The obligatory history was taken, and I got another opportunity to tell new medical practitioners that actually, no, I wasn't asthmatic. The transfer had taken an hour and a half. Pain control was starting to slip. There was a brief period of anxiety but before I was climbing the walls, I was morphined up and trying to settle into my new home.

CHAPTER SEVEN

....so, it will all grow back then will it?

"Whoa! Someone catch that, I think we need it later!"

26th February
Day 17

IV TPN
IV PPI
Morphine injections on demand

Now I was installed in the Royal Free and the operation seemed likely, the sister contingent of the family MDT was coming down on Monday and visiting Tuesday. I was sure members of the hospital MDT will remember their visit fondly...

The Consultant team came around, the structure was the same as the Alex: Consultant, registrar and rotating junior doctor and WoW. The consultant this time was the leader of the team here, and the one that would be doing my operation if it went ahead.

I have to admit, I became a bit of a fan boy of the consultant. It was not so much that he had a good bedside manner (whatever the hell that is), rather that he genuinely cared and tried to put me at ease. He did all this whilst actually answering questions, even if the answers to the questions were challenging or uncomfortable. He talked to you, not at you. Big fan.

He told me they were trying to organise the PET scan for Monday or Tuesday, this was still worrying me a lot. If the PET scan lit up, no operation. I did not say anything, mainly as there was nothing really to say. Just needed for it to run its course.

He ordered an X-Ray to review the positioning of the PICC line. Now while I am sure this was just a good medical protocol; I can't help thinking they did it so they could look at the line that "The Alex" put in and say things like 'look at the state of that' and 'what cowboy did you get to put that in?' while shaking their heads and chuckling.

He did leave me with one sobering point. Up to now, the medical teams had been careful to keep the options open regarding what the mass actually was. He did not. He told me clearly, but considerately, that the mass in his view and experience was definitely cancer.

The team left, leaving instructions to restart the various drugs, pain relief already in place.

The consultants cancer confirmation did trigger my emotional side, allowing my dark passenger to take control for a little while. Back to staring blankly, not able to talk, text my sisters or Debs - worried the hell out of them. I did get back to even fairly quickly this time and once I did, I found I actually felt better for the clarity. So much easier to face it.

I did manage to discuss with the family MDT medical director John and explained that I was still oscillating between "the cancer is contained" and "it is not contained and has spread all over the place".

He understood, 'A perfectly reasonable set of non-reconcilable divergent opinions'. He advised that someone once said the ability to hold two contradictory views is the sign of true intelligence but sucks to be me. It helped. The prick.

I was back in control by the time Debs came in bringing the supplies. It was an hour and half journey now, three-hour round trip. Never had one comment from her about it, across the whole stay.

We talked through the transfer and what we hoped would happen in the next few days. We had been so focussed on trying to get here, we had not given much thought to what happened next.

Things were gathering pace and it was just as well. Before she left, Debs noticed that my eyes had now gone yellow. The jaundice threatened a few days ago had arrived, accompanied by ever increasing levels of pain.

Day 18
IV TPN
IV PPI
Oral Morphine

No visits today. Debs had a bit of a cold and did not want to risk giving it to me, probably a blessing really. She had been running around so much after me while trying to keep all the other plates in the air, a day without travel would help.

The consultant round confirmed the PET scan was scheduled for tomorrow. The consultant, I think, realised I was really worried about this. He confirmed that from what he had seen of the other scans, if they did not manage to get the PET booked in and a surgical slot came up, they would go forward without the PET. That was a big relief.

While they were waiting for the PET and the theatre slot, they would start the preparation for the operation. Things were really starting to gather pace.

I was moved from morphine injections to oral morphine, apparently it could be absorbed in the mouth and throat. One less injection, so fine with me.

The anaesthetist came around that afternoon and explained what would happen on the day. I would be taken down to receive an injection in my spine for regional pain relief. After that, the next thing I would know would be waking up in ICU. I should be ready for some new additions, I will have some central lines in my neck, I would have an NG tube in, a catheter, two drains and an oxygen feed. Phew, glad she warned me.

Later, I passed all this back to John. As an anaesthetist himself, he was less interested in advising me and more interested in the specifics of the approach: telling me to check what regional anaesthesia they were going for, talking about TAP blocks, all sorts of nonsense. He was like a trainspotter who I had told I was getting on the Flying Scotsman.

I started to go through the history with the anaesthetist, which as you would expect was rigorous. given the scale of the operation it needed to be and yes, I had to tell them again I was not actually asthmatic....

Day 19

IV TPN
IV PPI
Oral Morphine
PET Scan

JOE DAINTY

PET day.

I was wheeled down to the imaging centre, backwards again if you are interested. The way the scan works is that they inject you with a small amount of radioactive material, you sit and wait for that to make it around your system, and then they scan. Areas of high metabolism are highlighted by the radiotracer; cancers are areas of high metabolism activity so they show up.

It all went without a hitch. The only real issue was it was bloody chilly down there and I was only in my hospital PJs. I was sitting there for thirty minutes with my teeth chattering, freezing my bits off, should have brought my blankie.

Debs was able to come in that afternoon, my sisters were also travelling down from Liverpool and joined us later. Not long after Debs came in the consultant popped around, this was before my sisters arrived. He had already reviewed the results of the PET scan and confirmed that while the mass lit up like a Christmas tree, there were no other sites. This indicated that the cancer showed no signs of having spread and the operation can go ahead.

The relief was immense. This now opened the gateway to a much better outcome of pancreatic cancer - much, much better. It allows us an option that over eighty-five people in a hundred unfortunately do not get, I think we both had tears in our eyes.

He asked if we would like him to walk through the operation with us. I realised then that I didn't really have any idea what the operation, that I wanted so desperately, actually entailed - beyond cutting the mass out. We accepted his offer gratefully and he begin to draw it out on a piece of paper.

The official title of the operation is a "pancreaticoduodenectomy", which is ludicrous and should only be used in medical exams. It is commonly known as a "Whipple" procedure.

During the operation, the surgeon will remove the head of the pancreas (this is where the mass has formed), the gallbladder, the upper part of the duodenum (small intestine), part of the stomach, part of the bile duct and surrounding lymph nodes. Once that is all done the pancreas and stomach are reattached to (what is left of) the small intestine.

Blimey.

So fair to say a biggish operation, apparently not many other abdominal operations are bigger or more complex. It will take 5-8 hours surgery, involving more hands in me than a tall racehorse.

Blimey.

We were fairly quiet after that. He confirmed that this was the only operation he had planned tomorrow (you could do something else on the same day?) and wished us all the best. It was very reassuring knowing he was going to be leading this, taking the time to go through this made a big difference to us.

My sisters arrived shortly after but missed him, we all talked about tomorrow and how ready we are and how glad we all were that it was going to happen. There was an undercurrent of worry and concern, but it was low. We were playing for big stakes and the risk of the operation was minor concerned to not having it.

It was happening just in time as well. It was not just my eyes that were yellow now, I was. Jaundice was fully formed now, and the abdominal pain was reaching the limit of the current morphine dose.

They left, wishing me luck, and giving me their love. I started to settle down and try to get a little sleep for the last time with all my guts still on the inside.

Day 20
Whipple Procedure
All sorts of drugs

Slept for a couple of hours, no more. Sat and watched the sun come up, listening as the hospital gradually came to life. I was just waiting to hear if the team had managed to secure an ICU bed for recovery, if not there would be no operation. This may seem odd, but it does make sense. If someone comes in overnight whose need is greater than mine for an ICU space then they get it, triage is what it is about.

The anaesthetist came up, the bed had been secured and I was going down.

I had given some thought to the risks of the operation; they were relatively low but always present given the complexity. I sent a note to Debs telling her I would see her in recovery, but nothing mattered more that her and the kids. I let John know and thanked him for his help, then I was into the wheelchair and off we went.

I entered a very busy room indeed and hopped up onto the bed. All sorts of preparations were going on: checklists were being read out; confirmations were being asked for and received; machinery was being pulled into play; packs were being opened. It was full on, and I was causing it.

The anaesthetist came over to me and walked through things again. She made sure I understood and did some last double checks I was actually me. I was rolled onto my side and the needle went into my spine. These guys were good, did not feel a thing. Some other drug was pushed into the cannula, and it all drifted away....

I came to. It was dim and quiet. I could just about see people moving around in the gloom, having whispered conversations. One was next to me but before I could speak, I was off again.

Awareness floated back, felt a little more awake but not much. I felt nothing, no pain but very little sensation at all - very disconnected. There was a nurse taking my vitals next to me and I was hooked up to various machines and could feel the tube in my nose. Suddenly I had a phone next to my head.

"You alright love? It's all done, you are out" it was my sister, Jan. Apparently, she was with Debs and Polly and had been ringing fairly non-stop since the consultant contacted them to say I was out after 8 hours of surgery. The staff got so fed up they decided to give me the phone to see if I could get her off their back.

"It's gone well love, really well, are you ok?" It was all a bit odd. Just out of major surgery, still high as a kite, and having a little chin wag with your sis whilst a nurse holds the phone on your ear.

"Did they get it all, I don't know, did they get it all?" I think that is what I said. I know the only thing I asked was if they had managed to remove all the mass. Jan's voice broke a little, may have been the connection, as she told me "Yes, they got it all".

The phone was taken away and I drifted back to unconsciousness.

CHAPTER EIGHT

Stitched up like a kipper, don't drink the coffee...

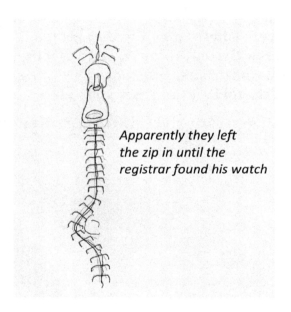

Apparently they left the zip in until the registrar found his watch

2nd March
Day 21

All sorts of drugs

The day after the operation I was judged fit enough to go back to the ward, don't remember much about the transfer back or most of the morning to be honest.

I could not really move to begin with, very warm and fuzzy. I had a control to self-administer additional pain relief and I used it liberally, whether I needed it or not, I was not taking any chances. Pretty much as soon as I arrived, the oxygen was taken out as was my catheter.

A chap came around from the occupational health team, he seemed very nice, and I was nodding along nicely when I suddenly realised, he was asking me to get up and walk. Did he not know I had just had major complex surgery? Ah, apparently he did and still wanted me to get up. Bugger.

This should be fun. I slowly swung my legs off the bed and tried to stand, still had pain killers flushing through the system so pain level was low, but boy was I weak. I leaned heavily on the IV stand and stood up - sort of. I could not see the wound as it was under dressing, but it pulled me into a curve making things a little difficult. I could feel dull explosions going off in that area, I suspect these would have flattened me without the pain killers.

I began to walk, well shuffle. The nice man from occupational health wanted me to go to the end of the ward and back. He suddenly did not seem so nice anymore. I hate him. Bastard.

It wasn't pretty, it wasn't quick and do not think either foot left the floor, but I did it and was helped back into bed. I swear if he started to talk about posture, I would swing for him. That was quite enough for today, cheery bloke left warmly confirming he would be back in a few days to see how I was getting on.

Debs and my sisters arrived, which was a wonderful sight. Straight into hugs and tears and chats and more hugs, took a while to settle down.

I could not tell them much of the operation from my side, I remembered speaking to Jan but that was about it for yesterday. They got a call from the consultant around 5pm to say the operation had been a success. Every indication was that the cancer was contained and they had removed it all. They needed the results of the biopsies to be sure, but they were as confident as they could be.

They had then started calling the ward for updates on me, until the team got so fed up, they passed them to me - the rest we know.

I was still pretty weak and finding it a little difficult to concentrate, self-medication was still a major feature. Jan noticed I was still lying on the pad that they had used in ICU and still in the same gown.

This did not sit well with what she thought should have happened since I arrived in the ward, and she left to have a 'word' with the team. I had the presence of mind to get her to leave her cosh and knuckledusters on the table.

A lot of people still wanted to come in and see me. Debs had been fielding all the requests and spoke for a while about when we could fit them in. If anything, it may give Debs a break from the travel as I'm still likely to be in for a little while yet.

Jan came back with some fresh pyjamas, a bowl of warm water, soap, towels, and sheets. She and Polly then proceeded to give me a bed bath. It was a tender moment, they are both experts in this, pretty moving having your sisters look after you like this.

After this, it was on with the new PJs which was like a game of twister, given all the tubes, IV feeds and drains but they achieved it with a minimum of fuss and pain. Ditto the sheets, still not sure how they managed that without me leaving the bed, definitely involved some rolling.

They also worked some sort of voodoo nurse magic with the pillows, so it was so much more comfortable, a sort of upside down 'V' with another across the top. God but I felt better after that all that, especially feeling clean again.

The magic pain button had been removed and pain awareness was coming back but did not seem too bad. There were certain things I could not do due to pain, but generally manageable.

Sleep was even harder to come by than it was before the operation. I have slept on my side ever since childhood, the wound and drains meant I had to lie on my back. It's not a position I could normally sleep in, but sheer exhaustion allowed me to. Eventually.

One of my fellow inmates decided they wanted to watch the television at 1am in the morning, stood it for a while but ended up shouting at him to switch it off or put his headphones in. A little voice came back that the headphones 'hurt his ears'. Afraid I responded that I could not really give a shit, trying to sleep, switch the bloody thing off! A brief pause and off it went...

Day 22

PPI
Blood thinner injection
Pancreatic enzyme injection
IV paracetamol
NG tube removed
Dressing removed

We had a bit of change of routine with the consultant round today. There was not a consultant but a rather bouncy registrar with the junior doctor and WoW. He may have been a consultant but just didn't look like it to me. I spoke to John about him later and he said he was probably a registrar with a couple of years under his belt, where often 'their confidence is higher than competency'. Oh good.

The registrar was full of enthusiasm and, well, loud. He was firing questions; assume they were rhetoric as not sure he heard the answers to any of them. He told me how well I was doing, prodded me a bit, had a look at the drain output, not too bad apparently, a bit 'biley' – is that a word?

He decided that we could take the NG tube out. Almost before he'd finished saying it, he was pulling it out of my nose - like a magician performing the 'string of handkerchiefs' trick. This was not painful, but it was not pleasant. It was a thick plastic tube about half a centimetre in diameter being pulled out of my stomach, up my throat and out of my nose.

He left throwing statements behind him as he went, indicating the dressing on the wound could also be removed, I could be placed on a clear liquid diet, he would look at the drains tomorrow, put me back on IV paracetamol to control pain now the bile duct was cleared. I missed the rest as he passed out of earshot, but he was still going.

The nurse came to remove the dressing over the wound. I am told the removal of waterproof dressing is akin to the pain level of waxing. If that is the case and I was a woman, I can assure you I would have very hairy legs as the removal of it felt like my skin was going with it.

So had the first view of the wound. I had given a lot of thought for the operation, I had not given any thought to the entry site.

Christ.

I looked down to a row of staples, starting at sternum and going all the way down to under my pyjama bottoms. I cautiously lifted the waistband, and they did stop fairly soon down there, which was good.

I counted the staples and there was about 40 to 50 of them. They looked like normal staples, I felt like a piece of upholstery. There would have been less staples, but they had taken a scenic route around the belly button.

Lots of dried blood and fluids obviously. Two drains which should not be considered tubes, more like pipes. They were big fuckers with bags at the end to collect fluids from the sites of major internal stitching – "bagpipes"? (sorry).

I carefully buttoned back-up my PJ top thinking I will leave all that for the moment, thank you.

The sisters came to visit bringing with them my nephew Joe. He works overseas at the moment and the fact that he had used one of his return trips to come and see me meant a lot. I showed them my wound, the sisters commented how neat it was. Jan wanted to see if they would let her take the staples out. Joe did not say much but looked a bit green, fair enough he is a quantity surveyor and not a healthcare professional. I felt a bit green too.

They did the magic with the pillows and left. I was still extremely tired and weak following the operation so could not really concentrate for long periods, so visits were a bit short.

I started on clear fluids. This was basically any fluid really, had some orange juice and some clear soup. Felt really strange to actually swallow anything at all, the last time was over three weeks ago. You would think it would be wonderful, starting to eat again after so much time, but it wasn't really. It was hard work. I had no appetite and with the rearrangement of my digestive system it all felt a bit off. That and the soup was absolutely minging.

I knew however that eating was an important step to getting discharged so tried to take as much on board as I could, over the course of the afternoon and early evening managed about 350 ml before I had to stop.

As I had started on fluids, I had to have pancreatic enzyme injections. The pancreas would not be able to produce enough enzymes to break down the food so needed this to do the job.

By Christ, this one was painful. I had one every day for the remainder of my stay and I swore involuntarily every single time. A lot. It burnt like hell itself.

Day 23

PPI
Blood thinner injection
Pancreatic enzyme injection

IV paracetamol
NG tube re-inserted

Towards mid-morning started feeling a bit odd. My stomach, while it had been pretty much dormant during my stay, was starting to wake up. I could feel various gas movements and gurgling going on. This was good (I think) as it showed things were starting to work and all the reconnections were working.

But that was not it. I was feeling off, starting to have a hot and clammy feeling - although I was not running a temperature. This feeling continued to build over an hour or so, until I realised I was going to be sick and pressed the call button.

One of the nurse auxiliaries arrived and hurried off to get a basin, she came back just in time and off I went.

Vomiting three days after surgery was singularly the most painful thing that happened to me during my stay. By far. If I was not being sick, I am sure I would have fainted. When I was playing rugby, I managed during training to break all the small bones in my wrist as well as two bones in the forearm. That bloody hurt. This was worse.

The problem was, you see, that the operation had cut through my stomach muscles - all of them, right through. Now the staples were holding them together. Now you probably haven't given this much thought, but you sort of need stomach muscles to vomit. Like, really need them. They compress the stomach to push the stuff out.

So, as I started to be sick, the muscles tried to contract but could not. Instead, the raw ends of them pulled against the staples on both sides and the pain was off the chart. I instinctively wrapped my arms around my midsection to hold it, luckily the nurse was holding the basin.

I was projectile vomiting, screaming, crying, and trying to hold myself together. Who said men can't multi-task?

It did not last long; I filled the bowl which was quickly swapped for another before it started to tail off. By this time, I had brought up about a litre and a half. I started to see what it was, and it did not look good. It was a dark brown, viscous liquid that smelt very bad. Oh, what fresh hell was this? I mean the soup was bad but really?

The nurse auxiliary was looking a bit concerned and hurried off for reinforcements. Ward nurse returned to tell me this was 'old blood' commonly referred to as coffee grounds, and a lot of it. She had paged the registrar to come over and, in the interim, started the IV paracetamol feed early as the aftershock pain was very high.

He arrived, noticeably less bouncy than yesterday. He took a look at the coffee grounds. They were probably from the operation itself which would be ok, or it could mean a new bleed which would not be good - so they needed to monitor pretty carefully. I was put back onto two-hour observations, back to nil by mouth and they were going to reinsert the NG tube.

I pieced all that together later, at the time I was just hugging myself and waiting for the paracetamol to kick in.

If puking coffee grounds without the aid of stomach muscles was the most painful thing to happen during my stay, the re-insertion of the NG tube was the most unpleasant.

They started to feed up my nose and guide it down the back of my throat. As it is a ridiculously thick tube, it instantly triggers your gag reflex and triggers it hard. Gag reflex triggers the stomach muscles, and we know how that goes. More paracetamol please.

They were trying to get me to sip water so that I swallowed the pipe, rather than have it going into my mouth or lungs. It eventually went down after choking it out a couple of times. I was cursing the registrar who pulled it out yesterday.

All of this left me completely exhausted with splashes of vomit/

blood around the place. My sisters popped in to visit on the way back to Liverpool and 'had another word'. Soon I was in fresh PJs, washed and professionally propped up. God bless 'em.

I was exhausted and did not look great; it had taken whatever I had left out of me. I called Debs and told her to hold off visiting with the kids as I think seeing me in that state would scare the shit out of them and, to be honest, I needed to just rest.

I desperately needed some sleep, so on the advice of Jan I asked for a sleeping tablet to see if that would help. Took that and hoped for some shut eye.

Day 24

PPI
Blood thinner injection
Pancreatic enzyme injection
IV paracetamol
IV TPN
IV antibiotics
Sleeping tablet
Contrast CT Scan

The tablet did work, and I got some sleep. It knocked me out but only for a couple of hours. I would ask for a double dose tonight, but at least I had got some.

I was sent down for a contrast CT to check everything was ok, a dye was injected which would show up any blockages or leaks. This was pretty uneventful except the CT team could not use the central lines in my neck to inject the dye, I had three of them from the op, similar to the central line in my arm but into my neck vein which is that little bit scarier.

They tried to get a canula in, but my veins were no longer playing. My veins on both arms were sulking and had disappeared from sight. They tried 4 locations without any joy. I would normally whinge about the pain this brought, but after vomiting without stomach muscles I was pretty blasé about someone digging around with a needle.

I innocently suggested that as the nurses on the ward were able to inject using the central line, could they not call one down to do it? This seemed to be ignored, until about 15 minutes later a nurse came down to do exactly that. Of course, the best solution would be giving the CT team the 20-minute training to use the central line - but I digress.

Debs did come in today with Harry and Emily. This is the first time they had since me since the operation. Sure, it was a bit of a shock but they managed admirably, telling me how great I looked.

I asked Debs if she could help me wash and change into fresh PJs. I wanted to get back into that routine but was just too weak to do on my own. Of course she would.

She helped me shuffle to the bathroom, undress, and wash. I had to rest in a chair between each bit we washed, it was a nice moment between the two of us. I felt so much better for it and think Debs was glad to be able to do some practical help, in sickness and health indeed. This was probably my weakest point; everything was a real effort and my weight was still going down.

My back was starting to get really painful due to not really being able to move around as much, Debs went to work with the massage gun and it was a great relief. I had been trying to do it myself but could not really reach or hold the gun.

I asked Deb to cancel all the visits she had arranged; I was just too weak. The operation and the lack of sleep left it very difficult to concentrate, and I was liable to nodding off. I hope people realised it was not because I did not want to see them and did not appreciate their concern, I was just not up to it.

TPN was restarted as I had not had any nutrients for nearly a week. The NG tube had a bag connected to collect fluid. What came out was a disturbing black mixture of the last of the blood and bile, just grateful not to have thrown that up as well.

Now, the next bit... is a bit unpleasant and involves bodily functions. I said at the beginning, I would tell the whole story - so if you are a little squeamish, it's best to skip the next couple of paragraphs.

I started to feel I needed a bowel movement. Now this is important, and the doctors were watching out closely for it to happen. I felt it would be received as well as the sign of the white smoke when a new Pope is voted in. A bowel movement would indicate the digestive system is active from stomach to bottom and everything in-between. Even a fart would be welcomed with delight at this stage, apparently.

I did not want to use a commode, so shuffled my way to the bathroom. Something was definitely happening. It was a hard thing to do, mainly again due to not having any stomach muscles. It was back to holding myself together as I went through the motions - as it were. Painful, but nowhere as bad as the vomiting.

It was more blood, old and new. New blood being bright red rather than black but plenty of both.

I told the nurse when I got back, she called for the doctor, and I was scolded a bit as I should have asked for help - and they wanted to see it. I could help there, as I had taken pictures. This may seem strange but thought they might want to see them, given the fuss.

The registrar was disappointed, ever had someone disappointed at your poo? New one for me. This was a movement but pure blood no stool, which reignited the concern about bleed. They needed to see the results of the CT scan.

I had two other movements during the afternoon and early evening. Both moved more towards old blood, which decreased the level of concern.

CT results were back. They showed some fluid and gas around the head of the pancreas outside of the intestine, indicating a minor leak. They decided to treat with antibiotics to give any leak a chance to heal. IV was added that night.

They also found some fluid in the pelvic area. This is usual and there was not much there, they didn't really seem to be concerned about it. It did not show any sign of a new bleed and this was supported by most of output being old blood. That was good news, as they would probably have to open me back up to sort that.

CHAPTER NINE

Eat, walk, fart, poo, go home

6th March
Day 25

PPI
Blood thinner injection
Pancreatic enzyme injection
IV paracetamol
IV TPN
IV antibiotics
Sleeping tablet

I got the double strength sleeping tablet and it did help, allowing just over 3 hours of sleep with some light dozing during the early hours. This would be the pattern for the rest of the stay.

Had the doctor round and we were back to the full complement, including a consultant. We went through the activity over the weekend, with the consultant advising that she would not have taken the NG tube out. Got the impression it had been discussed in more detail with the registrar, as he was not bouncy at all.

We were at a place now where we were starting to look at a discharge approach. We had to ensure the leak was stopped, my infection markers were also up and these needed to be managed back down. I also had to show I could tolerate food and pass it successfully. So, focus would be on these things. It was good to be starting to talk about discharge.

They would restart me on clear fluids today and see how it goes. If no joy, they would consider suppositories to stimulate the digestive action. Might as well, it is about the only hole they have not been in so far...

I mentioned I also was having some pain in my ribs. They were fairly sore and I asked about it, mainly concerned because it felt muscular and I could not see how it was related to the operation. Ah, they said, that will be from where they bend my rib cage back to get better access. Nothing to worry about and, apart from the fairly disturbing image this generated, they were right. The pain soon passed.

Debs came in and helped me wash and change again, as well as giving my back a good going over with the massage gun. I won't mention it again, but Debs continued to do the washing and changing religiously until I could do it myself and massaged until I was discharged. Godsend.

Started the clear fluids with limited success. I would drink some tea and, after a brief pause, it would come back up the NG tube into the bag. I was hoping at least some of it was going through but it didn't look like it.

As I had cancelled the visits, I started a WhatsApp group with close friends and family - the ones that had been in touch with either Debs or me. This, at least, started giving them updates of how I was going.

John gave the first major update to explain the operation in layman's terms, which helped them all understand context. Then I gave infrequent updates on progress, the response and support was just great - another boost.

Day 26 - 29

PPI
Blood thinner injection
Pancreatic enzyme injection
IV TPN
IV antibiotics
Sleeping tablet
Oral Oxycodin

JOE DAINTY

I have a new neighbour.

He is refusing treatment. The lack of medication is getting confused during the evening, shouting at 2am that his wife is outside and they are not letting her in. Quite distressed.

Even when he did take the medication, he refused to go to bed and spent the whole day and night in his chair reading and re-reading the daily papers. This was messing him up as he had serious ulcers and they were not going to improve with the lack of circulation that the sitting was causing.

He had gradually moved his table, so it was covering access to the toilet door. On one of my shuffles over, getting a bit easier but still a massive effort, I asked him to move across so I could get in.

He seemed surprised and told me the other patients had been using the toilet in the corridor. I pointed out that maybe the other patients had not been cut from breastbone to bollock, so I was not going to go to the corridor. Perhaps I could use what little strength I had to help him move his fucking table out of the way.

He felt that would not be necessary and was, of course, happy to move across. In I went.

The digestive action was starting to fire a little now, we were seeing some movements. Mainly water but it was a start. Looks like some stuff was passing through the stomach. Over the next couple of days, it moved from liquid to explosive diarrhoea and even a poo that looked like a poo. Progress!

The syringe to empty the stomach was starting to come up empty so looked like more and more was going through.

My red bloods test came back stable so looks like all the blood that I saw was from the operation. No new bleed, which was good news. Unfortunately, the restart of the stomach function was causing severe abdominal pain so back on pain killers and stopping the paracetamol as it was not cutting it.

This time it was to be oral Oxycodin, so away from the heroin substitute and onto the drug that has crippled the USA with addiction. Don't want to get too used to this one either.

The wound was healing remarkably well, so the area of focus remains on sorting the leak and getting to solid food. They were looking to repeat the CT next week to see if leak was healing.

Debs was coming, once with the kids, keeping me updated with everything happening in the outside world and keeping going with washing and massaging. I was trying to walk more as another exit condition was that I must be mobile. Up to over 800 steps per day, still hanging onto a stand and dragging my feet. Still needed a collapse on the bed when I finished but I was gradually improving.

On day 29, managed to wash myself. The TPN switchover happened while Debs was not there so decided to have a good clean while I was tubeless. Took much longer but managed, after a fashion.

Day 30

PPI
Blood thinner injection
Pancreatic enzyme injection
IV TPN
IV antibiotics
Sleeping tablet
Oral Oxycodin
Drains removed
Central line removed

Our Claire came in to visit. I should explain for the non-scousers out there that 'our' refers to anyone of your family: our Jan, our Polly, our Claire, our Joe. I think it is a very warm way of referring to family and shows Liverpool was leading the way with personal pronouns before anyone got 'woke'.

She came bearing gifts of the Saturday papers and some boiled eggs. This was not random. I had requested them as they had moved me to start soft foods today. Sorry to say they saw the new blood results and moved just as quickly back to clear liquids as the inflammation markers were up again.

I only found out after I was discharged how worried they were about these markers when John went through the discharge notes. They really were all over the place and at times very high, I remained blissfully ignorant.

Claire had to take the eggs back, great to see her and conversation flowed fairly easy but I was still very foggy and weak.

The drains came out today and that was very, very odd. Really hard to describe the sensation. I have read about people being stabbed and not feeling anything till the blade came back out and I related it to that.

There was no pain but the sensation of something being slowly pulled out of you that should not be inside in the first place was just not right. They were long as well.

Jan was not happy that things seem to be hitting a plateau and was pushing the team to have a clear discharge plan. Failing that, to get some respite trips away from the hospital even if for a few hours. Probably more evident to Debs and my sisters but I was becoming fairly confused and institutionalised after 30 days as an in-patient.

The dressing on my central line was flapping about, kept trying to get it redressed but was one of those low-level things that never seemed to happen. I manged to grab some tape and do a botch job myself.

Once the nurse saw that, she decided it was time to take the lines out, I had basically sticky taped half my face and it was still falling off. No sensation to this at all, just 3 very long thin wires coming out of the side of my neck. Nice.

Day 31 - 32

PPI
Blood thinner injection
Pancreatic enzyme injection
IV TPN
IV antibiotics
Sleeping tablet
Oral Oxycodin

As the inflammation markers were moving about, I was frequently moving from soft foods to clear liquids and back again. I was struggling to get much down in any case due to the cramping pains and also constantly feeling full and having no appetite. When I was on soft foods, I was getting Debs to bring stuff in as it was just better and easier to eat.

The feeling full was due to a few factors. Digestion is sluggish after the operation, some of the nerves that told you if you are full have been removed or changed location. The stomach itself was resected, so could hold a little less.

No appetite was also common, just generally around surgery and being nil by mouth for so long.

Both of these issues will follow me home.

They decided they could give me everything orally or injected going forward, except TPN which had a dedicated line, so they removed the remaining canula. Later, on the shift change, they found out the antibiotics still needed to be via IV so needed to re-fit the canula and the person to do this would not be available till 1am that morning.

I completely lost it, for the first and last time during the stay, it just felt like a last straw. I bitched and moaned like a gud 'un, became one of the patients I had been taking the piss out of to my sisters. It did me no good at all, did not even make me feel better. I recovered enough to later apologise to the nurse I ranted at as not her fault.

Day 33 - 34

PPI
Blood thinner injection
Pancreatic enzyme injection
IV TPN
IV antibiotics
Sleeping tablet
Oral Oxycodin
Half Staples removed
NG Tube removed

The NG tube was coming out for the second time, this could have probably come out a couple of days earlier. I asked them to leave it until they were absolutely sure it would not be required. It was uncomfortable, but no way did I want that bastard re-inserted.

Well, they were sure now. So, a repeat of the magic hankie trick out of the nose. They also removed half the staples. Jan was in and you could see here itching to get hold of the tweezers.

They repeated the scan which showed the amount of gas and fluid had reduced, so looks like leak was healing or healed. There was still fluid in the pelvic area, got the impression they had no real idea how it got there. They did not seem that bothered, it was being medically managed with the equivalent of a Gallic shrug.

I was told I could move to eating solids if I could get on with this, it would just be the inflammation markers to manage to get the hell out of here.

Day 35

PPI
Blood thinner injection
Pancreatic enzyme injection
IV antibiotics
Sleeping tablet

Everything was starting to head in the right direction, but I was not getting excited until I was in the car.

The sisters had gone back and Debs' parents had come down to help keep the kids entertained while she was in visiting me, a long trip down from Scotland and much appreciated.

I had graduated to toast which was pretty solid, let me tell you. I had to dip it in the tea just to tear a bit off. I was eating pretty normal now, still really small portions as stomach could not handle heavy loads.

I was on a supplement called Ensure to fill in the gaps, gave you tons of protein and carbohydrates in a 25 ml pot. You guessed it, tasted disgusting. But if it helped me get closer to the exit, I can treat it like a bush tucker trial.

The TPN stopped as I was eating regularly. This meant they could use the line for antibiotics, so I was canula free for the first time since I was admitted.

Pain had decreased a lot. There was still cramping and bloating but it was manageable, so we stopped the pain relief which was, well, a relief. I was still paranoid I was risking going out with a developing addiction problem.

Still no appetite and constantly feeling full, but just pushed through with eating regardless.

Day 36

PPI
Blood thinner injection
Pancreatic enzyme injection
Sleeping tablet
Rest of staples removed.

They stopped the antibiotics yesterday. They wanted to keep me until tomorrow, just to make sure the inflammation markers remained down. They were happy with my mobility, I was up to

2,000 steps per day, in fact they told me to calm down a bit as I was wearing a hole in the lino.

During the consultant round they casually dropped in that they had the results of the biopsy. I had purposely not asked. I was focussed on recovery and did not really want to think about the implications of the operation itself until later, looks like this was later.

Firstly, they confirmed the mass they removed was cancer. It was still a slight shock to actually hear this. Despite every piece of evidence pointing that way. I was still holding out a tiny hope it was not.

Secondly, all the biopsies taken from around the site were free from cancer. Further, they had removed 42 lymph nodes as part of the mass and only 6 of them were cancerous. Apparently, this was a really good indicator. If it had not breached the majority of lymph nodes right next to the mass then it's highly unlikely that it had spread, especially with all other sites being clear.

Not sure I took all this in at the time. The consultant, the one who conducted the surgery, summarised for me: "We are very confident we got it all". A very sweet sentence indeed. However, there is no certainty here and pancreatic cancer is a real bastard, so clearly some chemotherapy looms in my not-too-distant future.

Debs' parents returned home and I told her not to come in, as I was hopefully getting discharged tomorrow. There was only one minor slip towards the end of the day, I vomited. Massively. I think I had just been pushing the food a bit hard to show I was ready. I decided not to tell anyone, best they don't worry – and I was not going to let it stop me getting out tomorrow.

Day 37

PPI
Removal of Central Line

The inflammation markers were still down, and I was going home! It did not feel real, I was excited but also a little scared.

There was a flurry of activity in the last hours of my stay. The last central line came out, they had left it until today, in case they needed to restart the antibiotics.

Next was sorting out the drugs to exit with. PPI and blood thinner will continue and added to that would be Creon, which are replacement pancreatic enzymes.

As a third of my pancreas had been removed it was not going to be great at producing these enzymes going forward. In addition, the triggers to say 'we need some enzymes, he has just inhaled a burger' were in the part of the duodenum they whipped out as well. These may recover over time, but unlikely. I was going to become very familiar with replacement enzymes.

While we were waiting for the pharmacy to issue the 1st set of drugs and to receive the discharge summary, I got dressed for the first time since I left the Alex.

When I started all this, I was over sixteen and a half stone. I was now under thirteen. I had some fat that went first, but also lost a lot of muscle mass as well. When I got dressed, I looked like I was playing dress up in my Dad's clothes.

The T-shirt was two sizes too big, and the waist of my trousers were six inches out. The belt was on its first notch, and it barely held them up. I looked bloody awful, even my shoes were loose. I suppose it was appropriate I looked like a refugee, after all I was being repatriated.

The drugs and report arrived, and I was off in my last wheelchair ride to the discharge lounge. For old times' sake we went backwards. I noticed the discharge report still said in history I was asthmatic, but written further down was 'the patient is not actually asthmatic'. Success!

JOE DAINTY

Debs was on her way, and I sat in the lounge, which was very pleasant. Comfy chair. I could see the outside world with people and everything.

I could not carry my bag. Not allowed any heavy lifting due to the wound, nothing to do with me not being able to lift it anyway.

Debs arrived and I was helped into the car, and we set off. We got about a mile before I started crying. More leaking really. I thought I might, big day and all that. Debs was a bit moist eyed as well and we sat in comfortable silence, holding hands.

We were going home.

EPILOGUE

It took a while to balance the enzymes, intervals between food, smaller portions, sluggish stomach, and there was a lot more vomiting, but we got there. They were expecting me to lose another 10% of my body weight after I got home but I have actually put on nearly a stone. That showed 'em.

Being able to sleep again was a real boost and I took and still taking, full advantage.

My niece Kate came down to stay and help us. She is studying to be a nurse and was a great help, especially with the blood thinner injections that neither Debs nor I fancied doing. She also cooked some great meals. Like a great tag team, nephew Joe also came down. He was great as well taking the kids out for breakfasts and lunches as well as keeping spirits up. Sisters were down as well, obviously. We are a close family, especially when it matters.

Started to have all the visits from friends that had built up over the inpatient stay. It was great to see people and, on balance, best I had waited till I got home. Some of the visits were fairly emotional still but would have been much harder if they had happened during my stay.

As I recovered, I was able to travel up to London to meet with the people I work with, especially my team. It was great to see them, to thank them for all the support they had given me and to show them I had come out the other side. I could not stay long as I still tire easily, but managed to stay long enough to have a gin and tonic…

The most emotional was when John and Gina 'popped over' to see us from Australia, during a conference trip to Europe. Probably did not look emotional to anyone else, but John and I knew.

Chemo has started now, 12 two-week cycles over 6 months. They still think they got it all, so this is more preventative and precautionary. You cannot mess with pancreatic cancer. You need to take all measures to improve your outcome, in my view.

I guess it would be useful to give a little bit of detail around the chemo. Usual caveat that it is different for everyone but think there are a lot of common elements.

I am given 4 main chemo drugs, three of them I give over one day as a day patient and I come home with a pump that dispenses the 4th over two days, then the pump is removed. You receive a lot of information about side effects and by Christ there are a lot that you can have, it is a thick pamphlet. Some sound scary as hell and can be very serious but are rare.

For me, the fatigue is far and away the biggest impact. On a two week cycle it completely wipes out most of the 1st week and remains as level of tiredness throughout, that said I have had a baseline tired of 50-year-old man with young kids for nearly decade now – but fatigue is a different ballgame.

It is zero energy. It is thinking about doing things but not getting them done, could be as simple as getting out of bed. It is dozing, it is losing track, it is failing of concentration, it is not really functioning.

You just have to let it happen and come out of it, as I said for me this is about a week and then just tired with low energy but able to function.

There are other side effects, loss of appetite, altered taste, some nerve pain. These are mild for me and again tend to fade towards the second week. When I look at the menu of side effects there are I am so grateful that I am having it relatively easy, this is reinforced when I am in as a day patient and see clearly what some of the other people are going through, 'lucky' seems an odd word to use here, but I am really.

I suppose it might be useful to list the main things I have learned during this. In the hope that it might help anyone who is in similar circumstances, either looking down the barrel of cancer or facing major abdominal surgery – or you may just be trying to help someone through.

Have to stress this is just my thoughts and views, it is by nature a very personal journey for everyone.

By far and away the hardest piece was handling the diagnosis. I fell to pieces, for a long period. I don't think you can prepare for it; you can only go through it. It does fade, although it feels like it never will, mainly because you cannot maintain that level of panic, emotion, or intensity. Over time, more positive responses have time to creep in, even if some of these are still pretty bleak.

I was lucky enough to go through it mainly with family and some close friends. It would have been a much, much more damaging experience for me if this support was not there. If you do not have anyone you can share with, still try and talk to someone.

I have not mentioned them here, as I spoke to them after discharge, but Macmillan cancer support are brilliant and always on your side.

The 'dark passenger' has moved from the back seat to the boot now, he may make a brief reappearance depending on how the scans go but think pretty much under control for the moment.

Perspectives change, now we are thinking more in terms of years than weeks or months we were during the in-patient stay. When you think about it, are we not always thinking in terms of years whether we realise it or not? You manage to pull the Big C to be part of the overall picture rather than just being the picture.

Working around the side effects, we have started getting back on with things, doing small trips, small tasks, and planning others –

there is a level of normality you can get back to while the future is unclear and that feels good. Of course, this all may be impacted by treatment or Big C developments but could also be swept off course by winning the lottery or tripping on a kerb, welcome back to uncertainty!

A lot of things I found out were related to the hospital stay itself.

You need to be involved, heavily involved, in your treatment plan. If you cannot face it, try to make sure someone is.

The medical team is trying to help you, of course they are. But they need to understand where you are, as there are often options. Seldom is it completely black and white. You can, and should, influence the treatment plan to where you think it should go.

Day-to-day on the ward, try not to sweat the small stuff. They are stretched and focusing on the big-ticket items. Constant triage of resources, scans and beds is continuously going on around you and treatment will often be delayed and bumped or happen without warning. It is just the way it is. That said, if you urgently need something – shout loud.

Don't let them switch the buzzer off.

Take all the pain relief they offer you. Don't worry, like me, about which ones they are using. They know what they are doing. You will have enough to contend with, without being in unnecessary pain, no need to tough it out.

Sleep deprivation is a fucking killer. Do everything you can to maximise a longish sleep at night. Dozing does not help, as you are not getting deep or 'REM' sleep so will still get all the tiredness, reduced mental capacity and grouchy with it. Tell people to turn their lights off, to switch their TV off, get the nurses to switch the main lights off - anything to increase your chance of sleep.

Buy some noise cancelling headphones if you can.

Above all, get home. Safe.

ACKNOWLEDGEMENTS

I have so many people to thank.

Debs, Emily, and Harry, they have been so brave through this and done all the heavy lifting. They are still guiding me through this today.

My family MDT, Jan, Polly, John and Steve, thanks for being there for me, making sure my spirits were up and I was getting the best treatment, for keeping me sane and keeping my dark passenger in the back seat. Thanks to all the other family members, especially Nonny and Grampy for being so supportive.

Thanks to 'our' Claire for the eggs and 'our' Louisa for the walk, you saw me in, you saw me at the out.

The teams in the Alex and the Royal Free, your dedication and skill is humbling. Thanks Anna…

Bill, Dex, Benoit, Texas Pete, Steve, Dom, Keren – thanks for staying in there and coming to see me, even if I was not the best company.

For all the encouraging messages (and a gin 'n' tonic) thanks to the best engagement team in the market, I won't list the names, but thinking about every one of you.

To everyone on the 'Tis But a Scratch' group, your encouraging messages always gave me a lift, they still do. Not to forget the Fat Boys, we will be raising a glass before you know it.

Thanks to everyone in the wider Blueprint family, across Lloyd's, the JV, the Associations and LIMOSS, for all the messages, cards, and gifts. You are proof when it matters, we are indeed one team.

Thanks Bob, a great boss, a great friend.

To John, Steve, Matt, and Charlotte for reviewing the drafts of this, not sure it made much sense before your council.

Finally, thanks to you for reading this, whether you enjoyed it or not, you have donated to Cancer Research UK and that is what matters.

Printed in Great Britain
by Amazon